Volume: 01

LICENSE FREE TATTOOS:

"TROUBLE IN ASIA"

BY: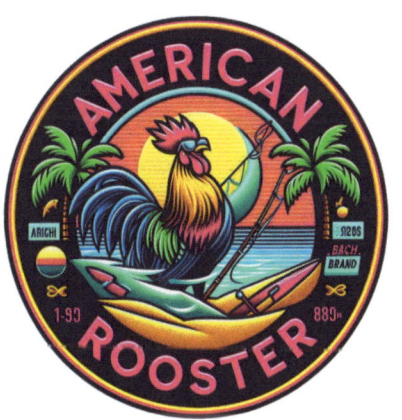

https://www.AmericanRooster.com

Hello Friend, please notice that we have included our QR code on each page. This is so that people can find us when the art is shared and people who benefit from the free-license can choose to support us with some merchandise purchases.

You may share the designs with your friends so long as our QR code is always present. Without the support of the people this project will not be sustainable and our plans for future volumes will die.

Elephant Section

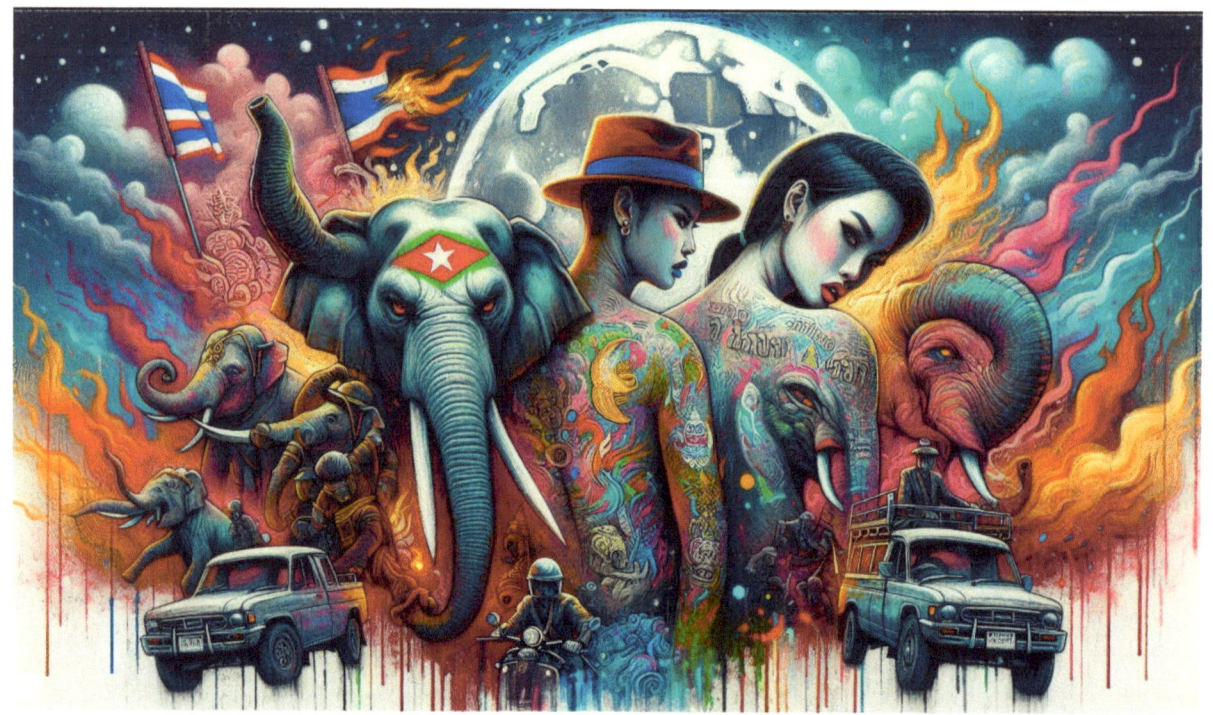

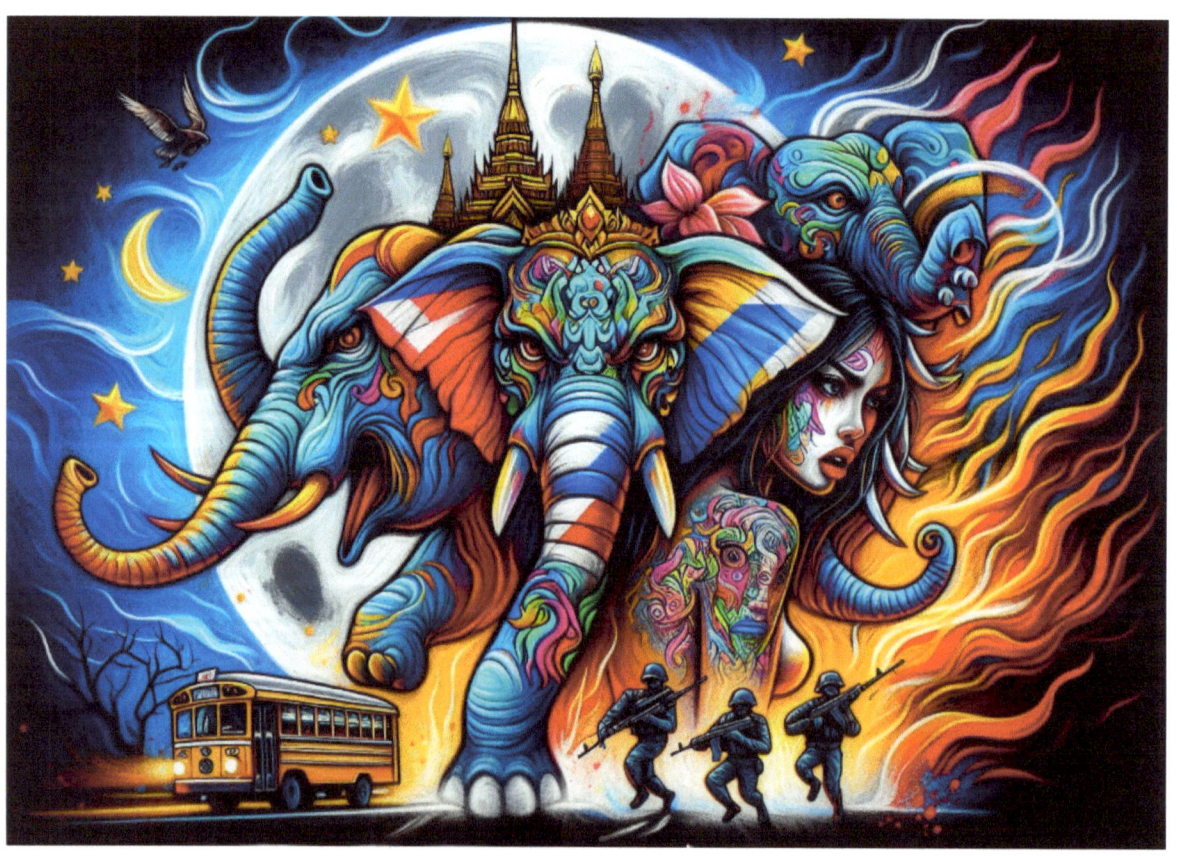

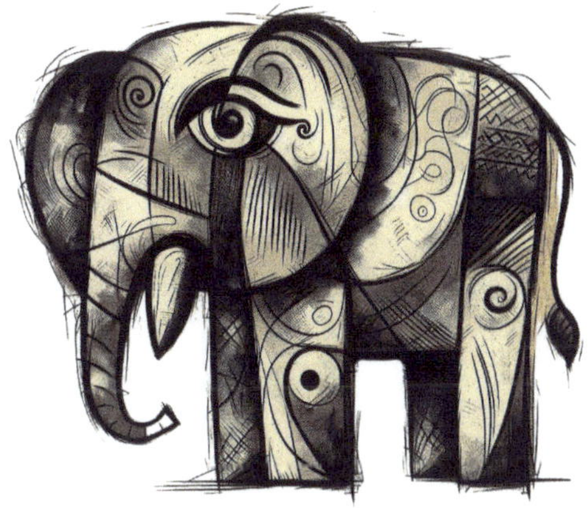

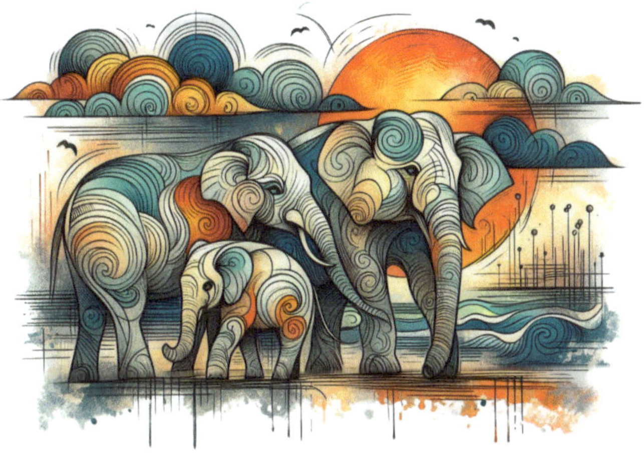

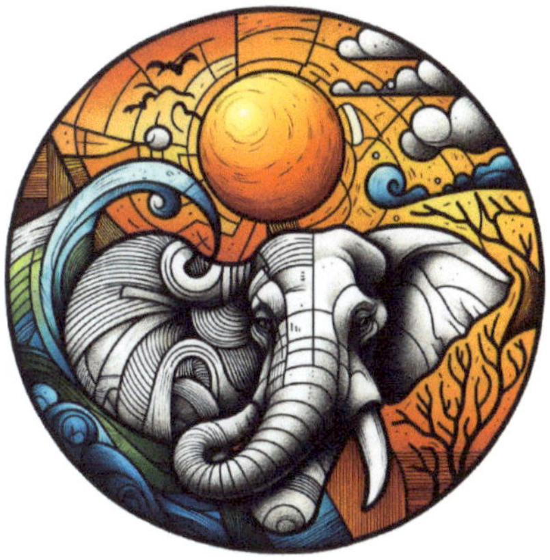

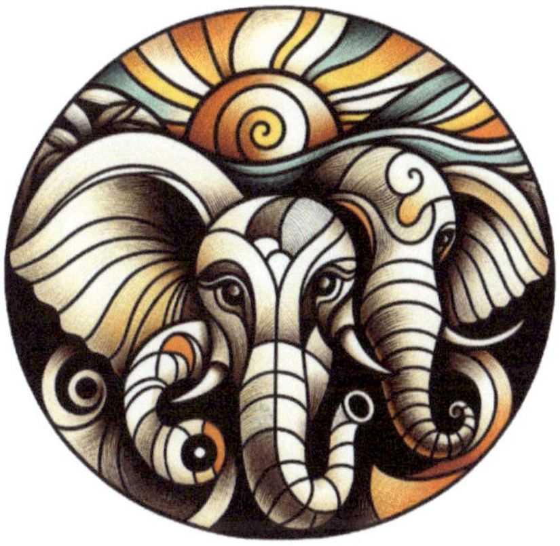

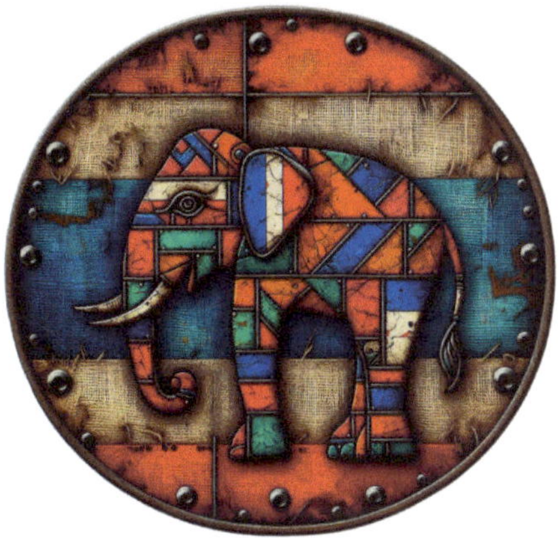

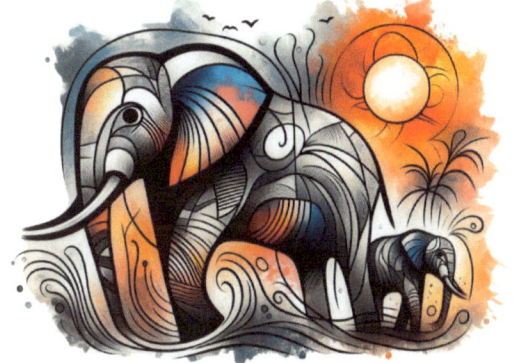

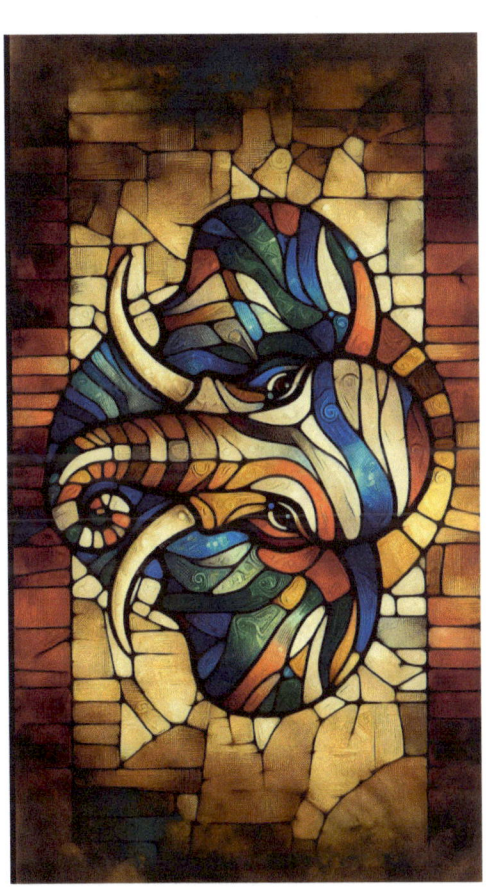
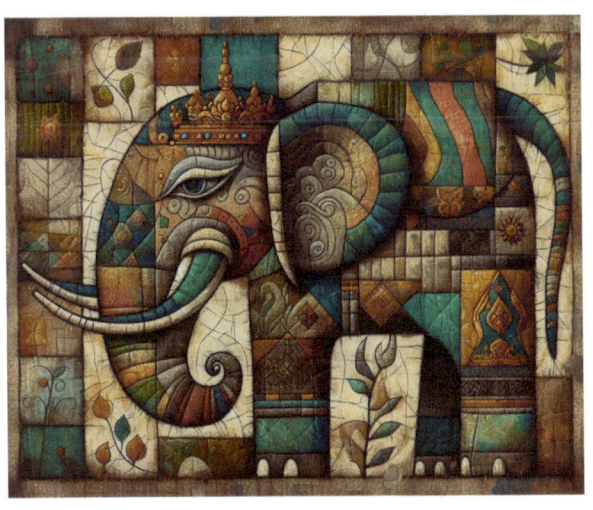

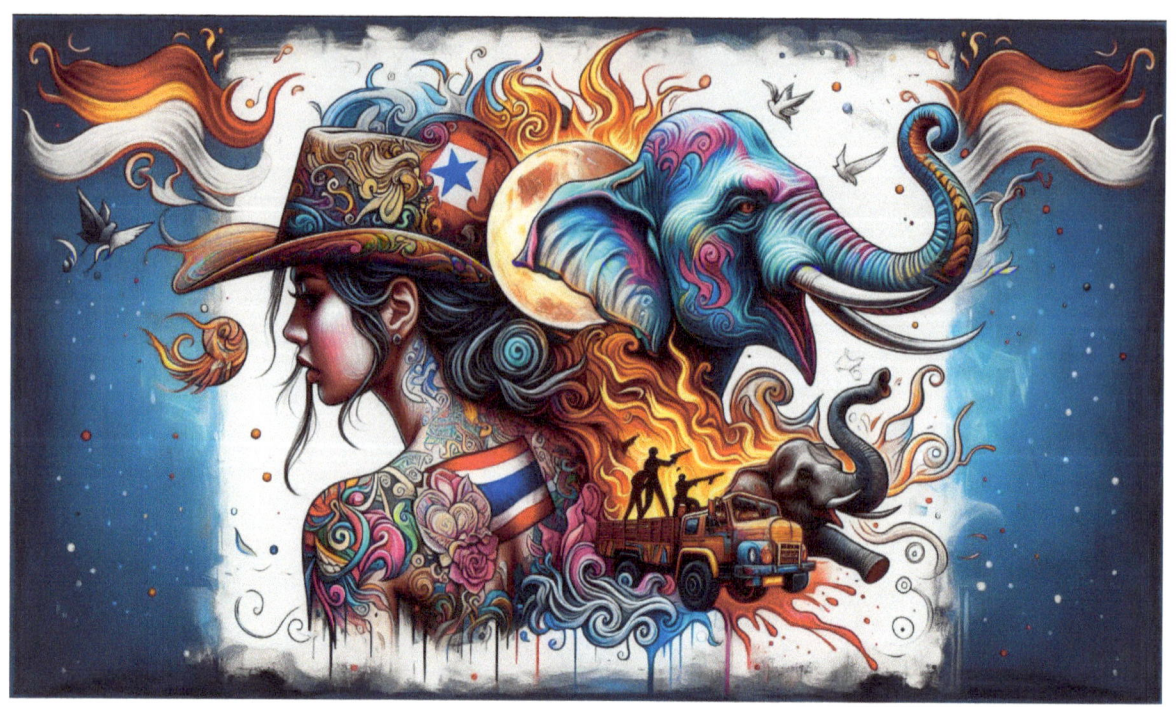

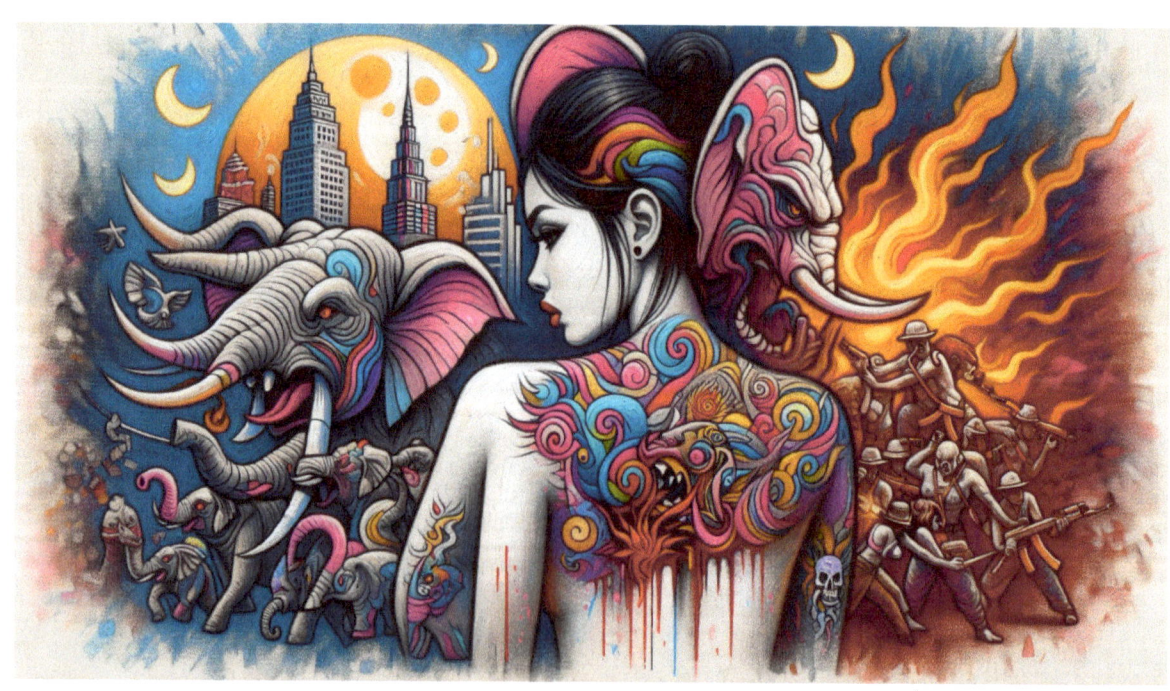

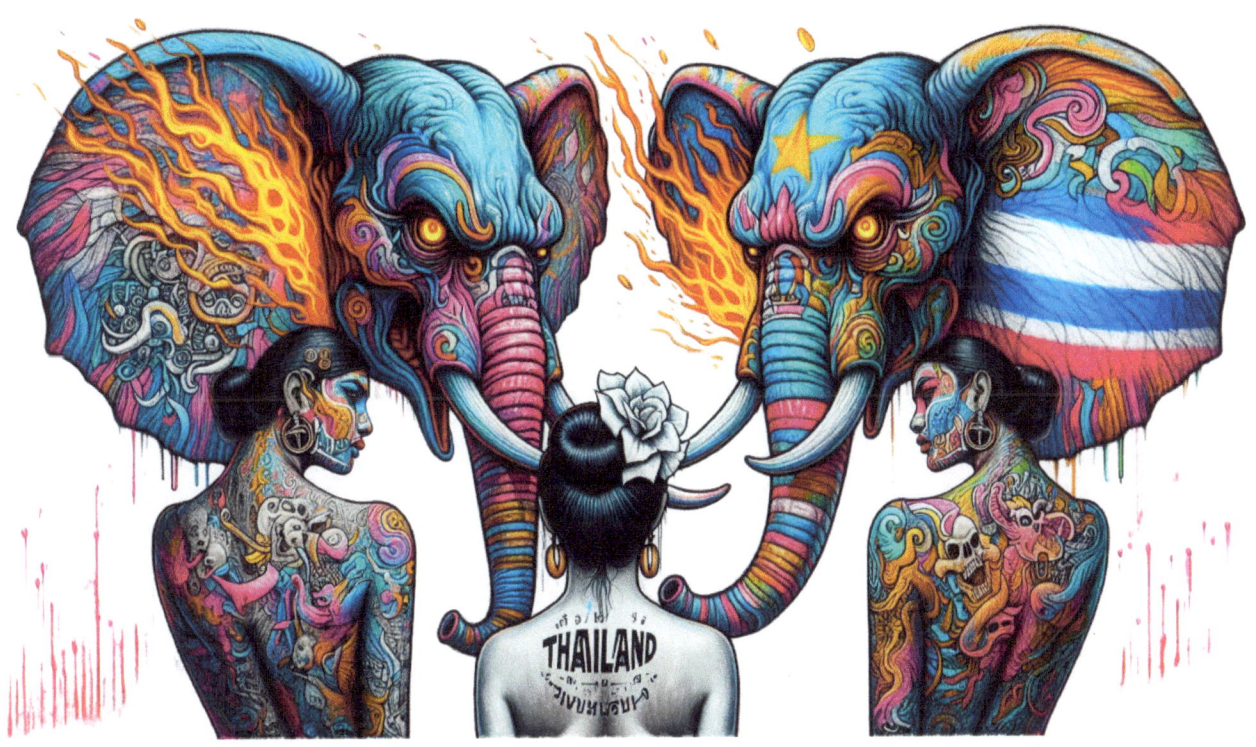

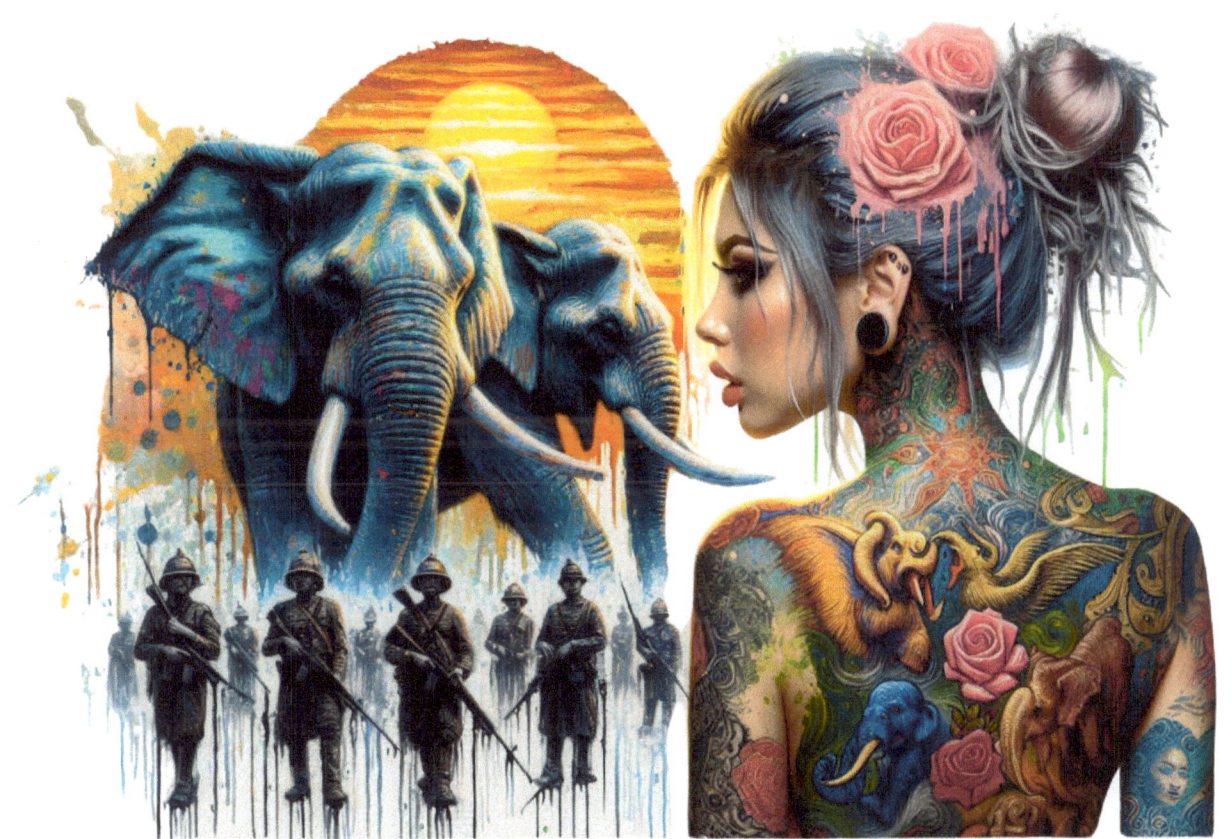

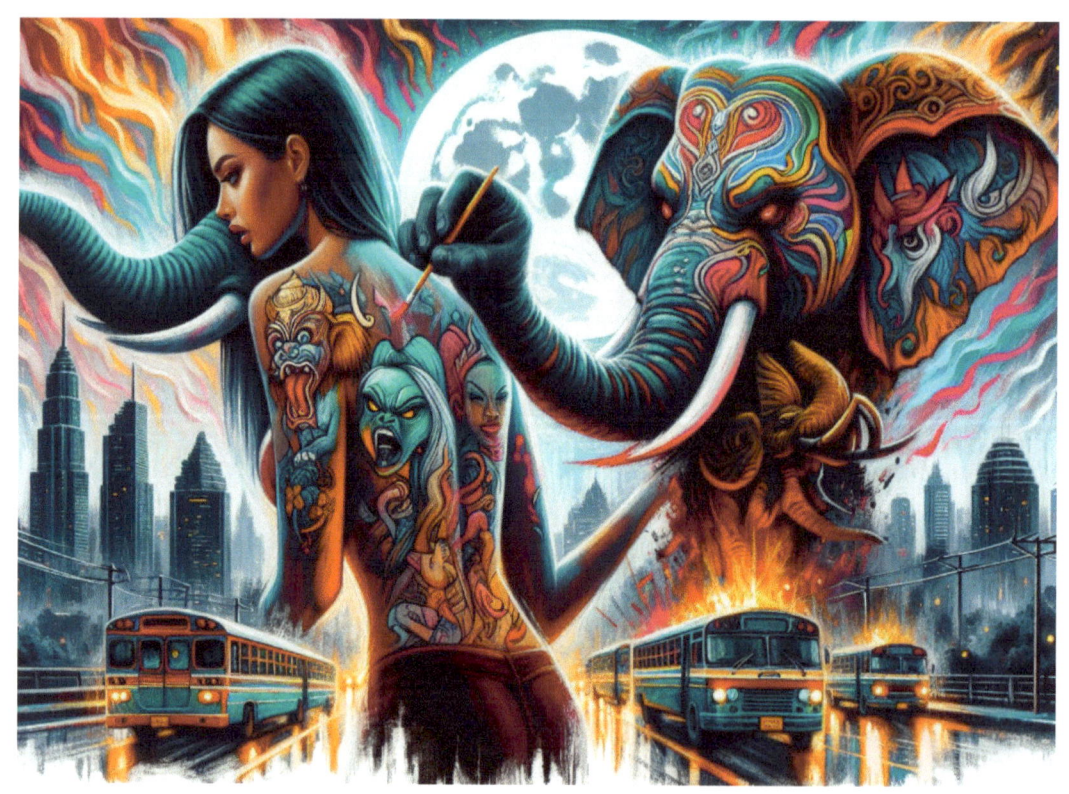

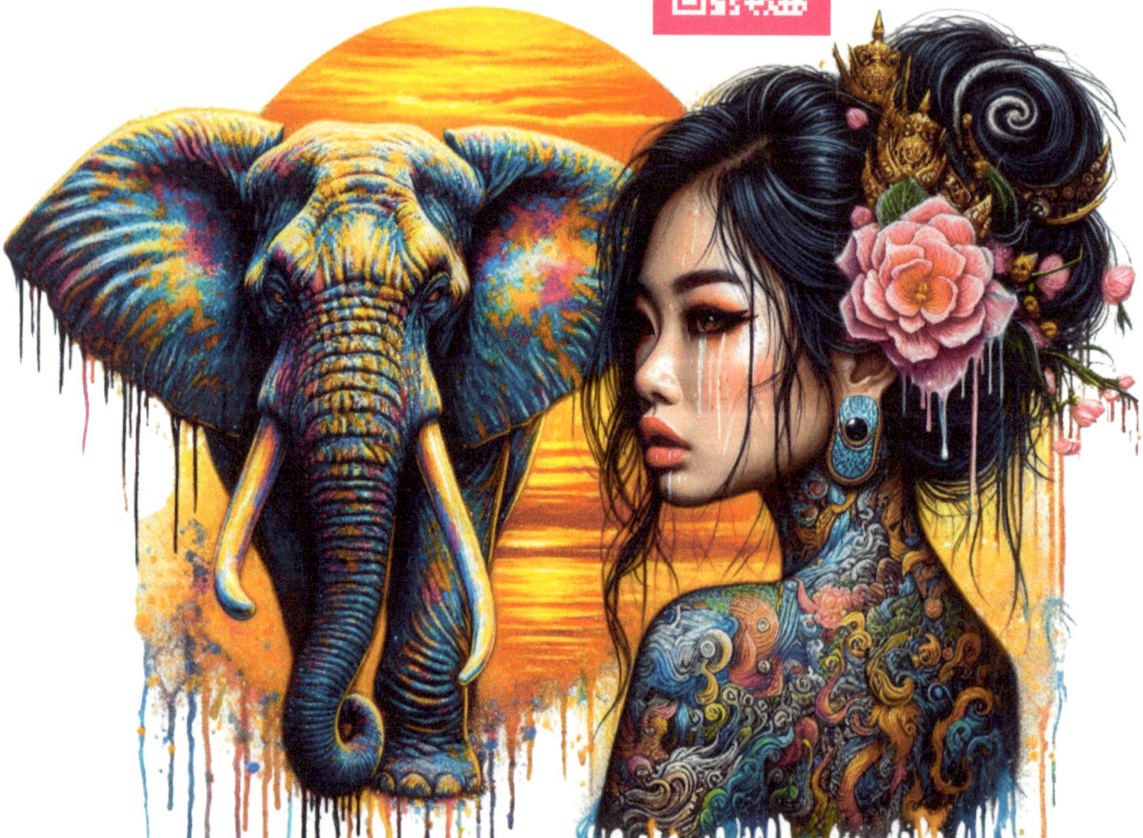

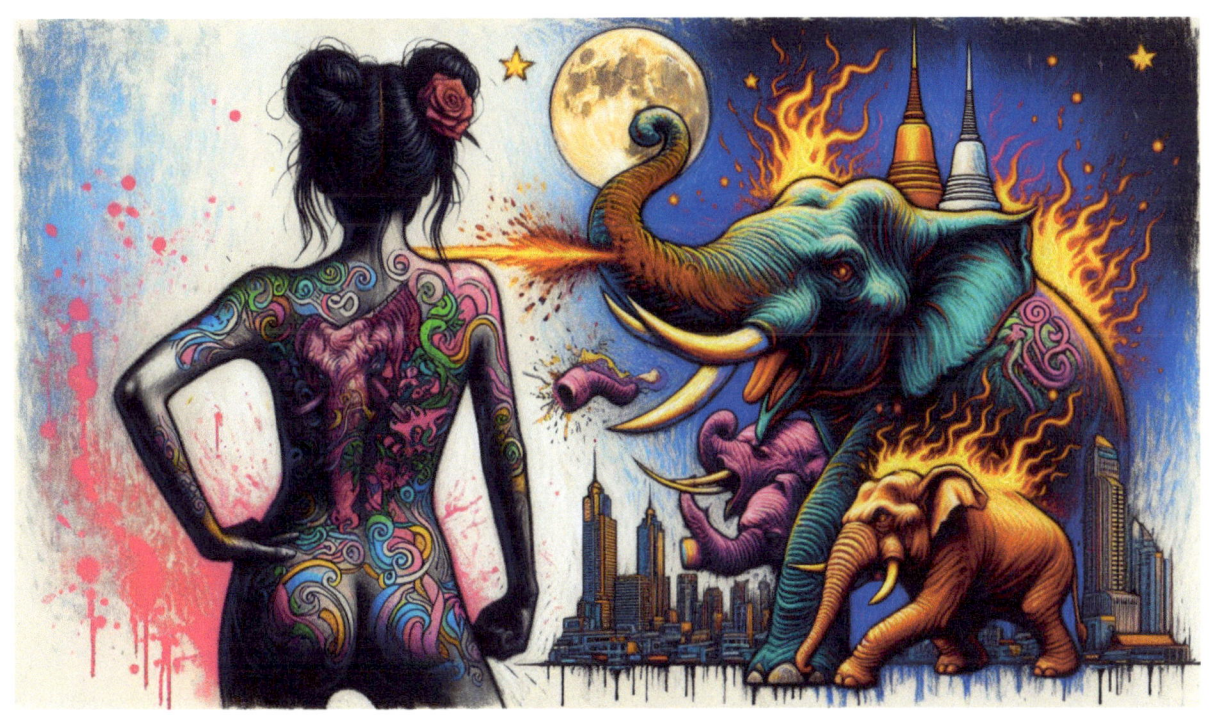

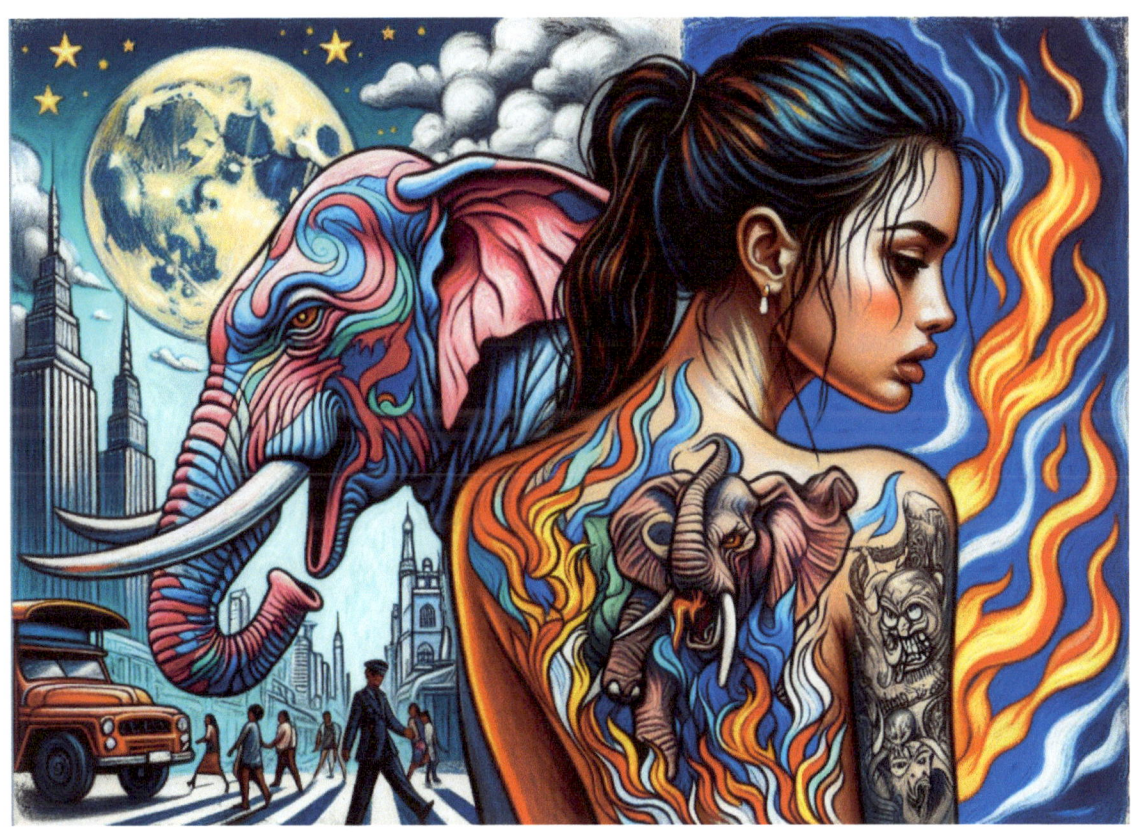

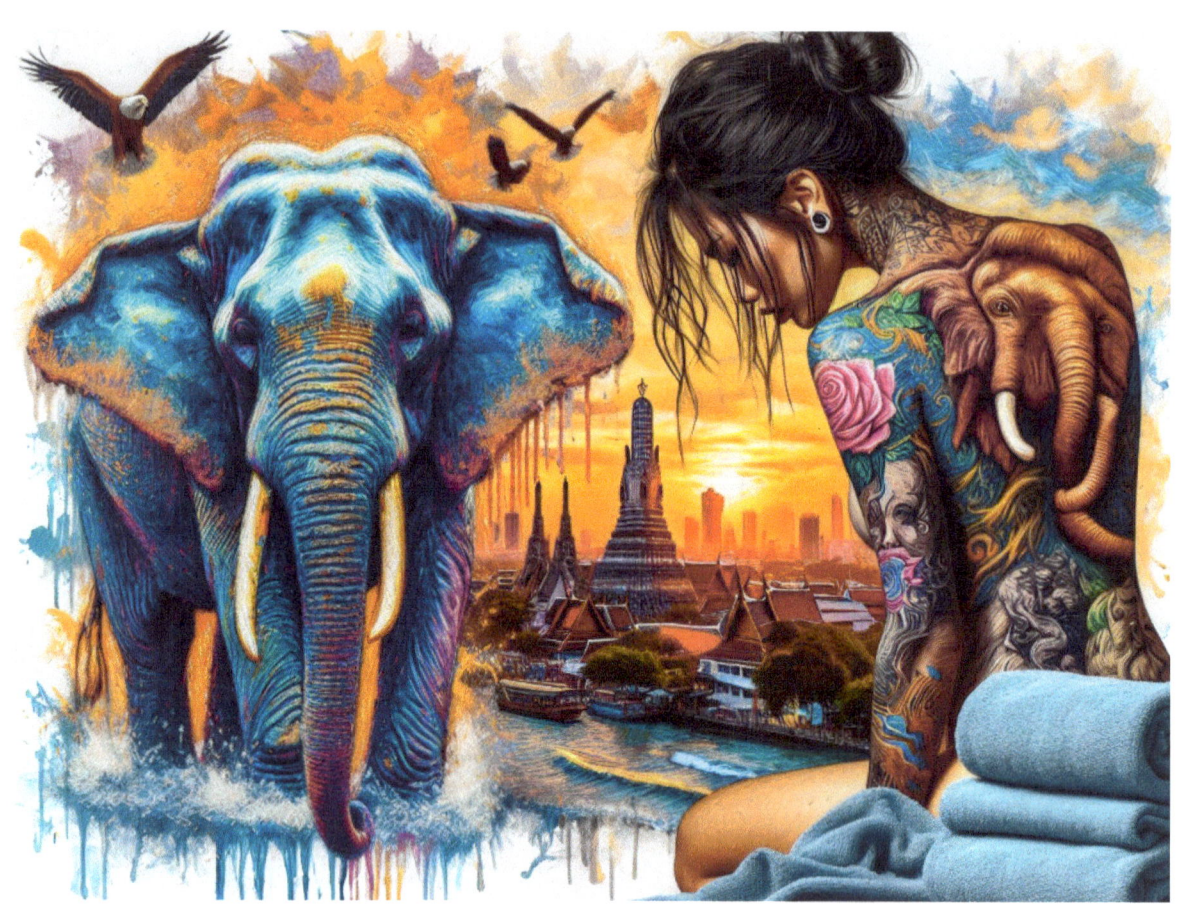

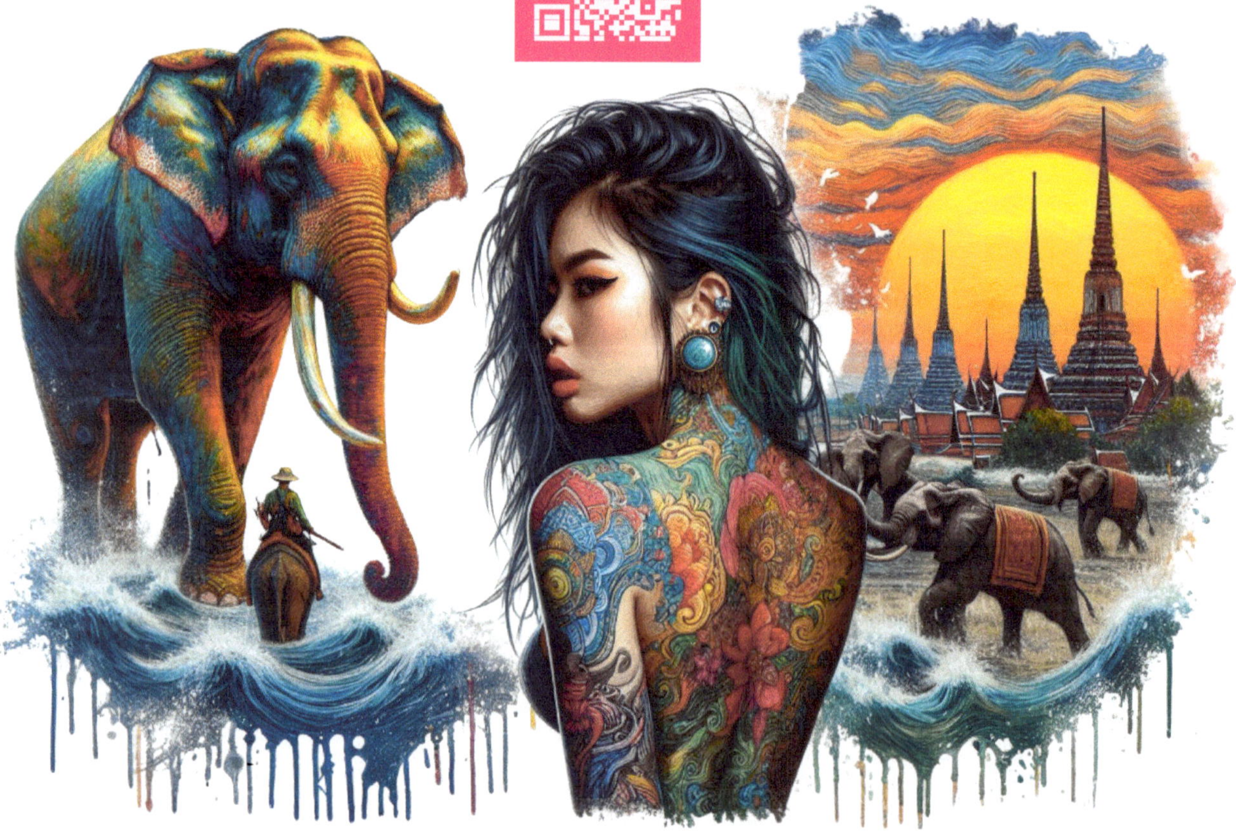

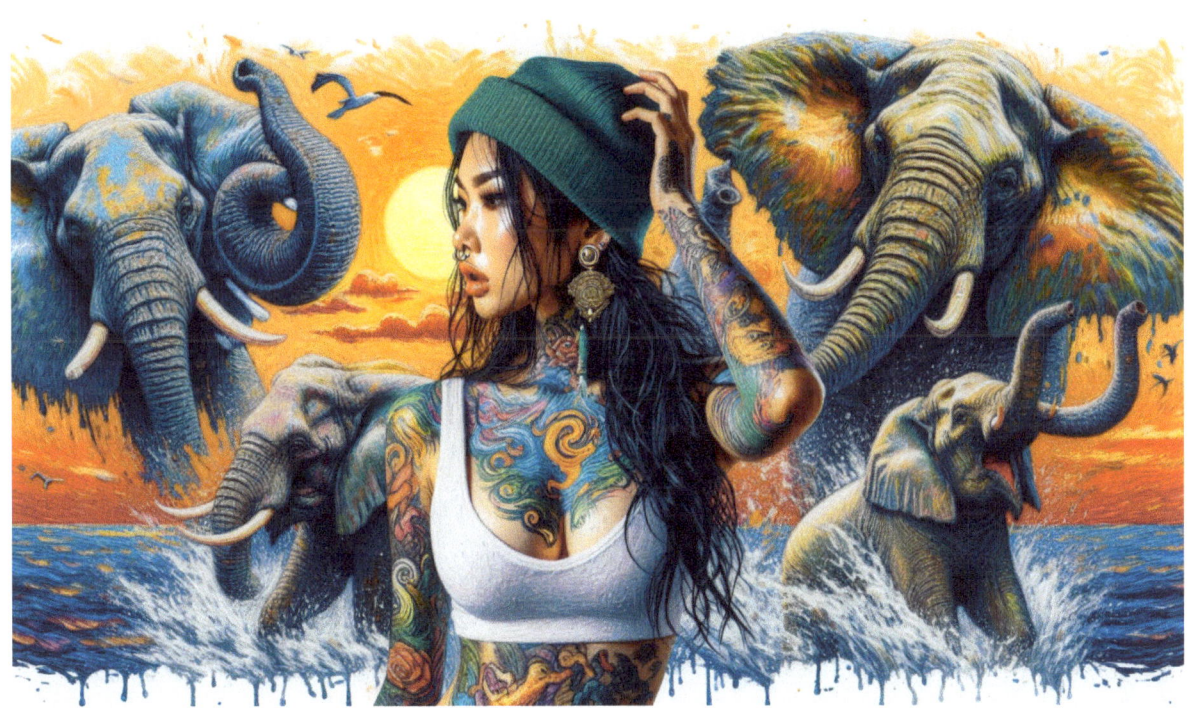

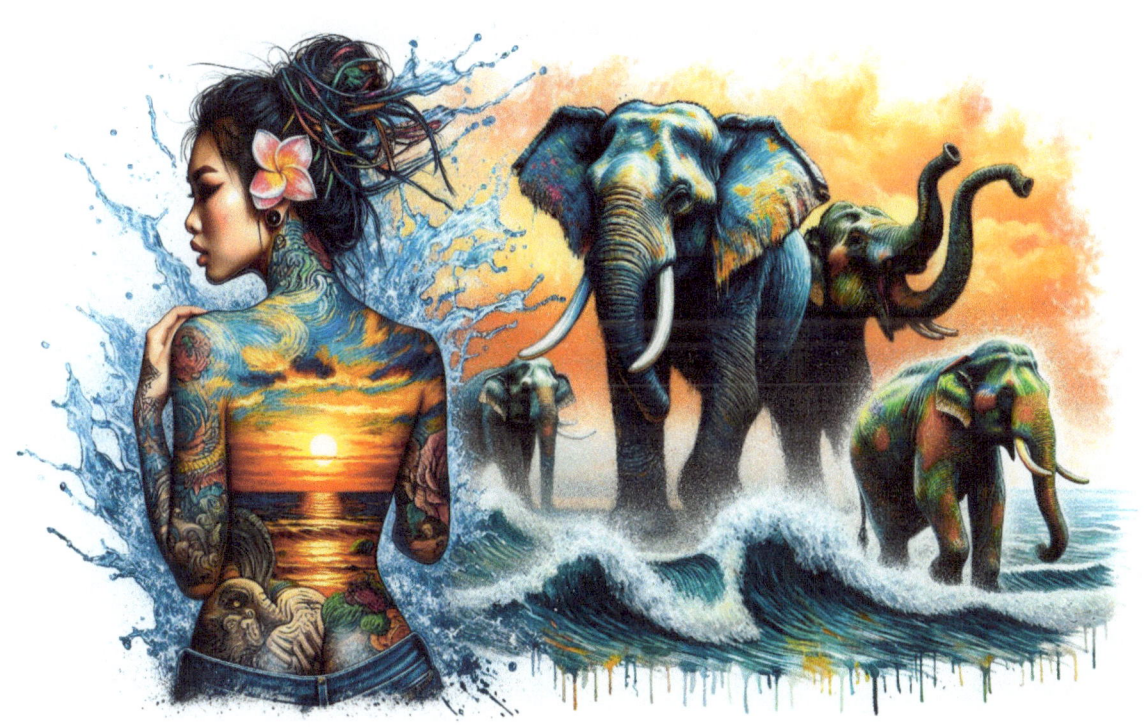

Rooster Section

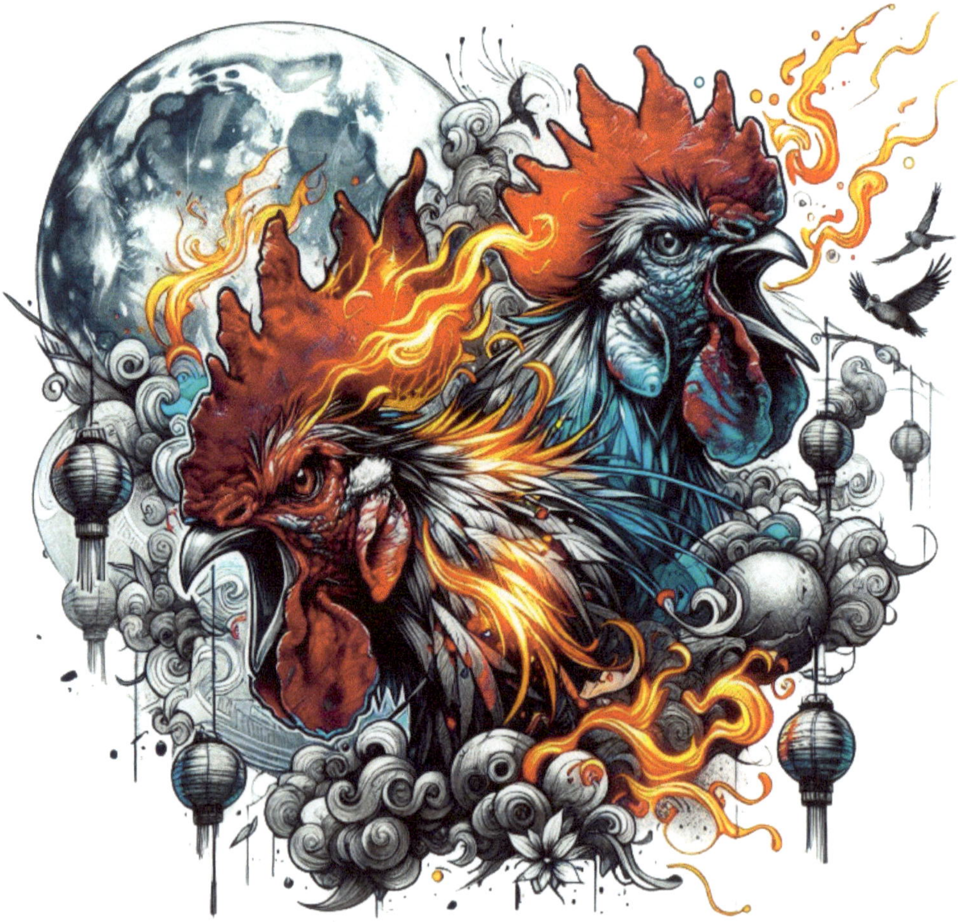

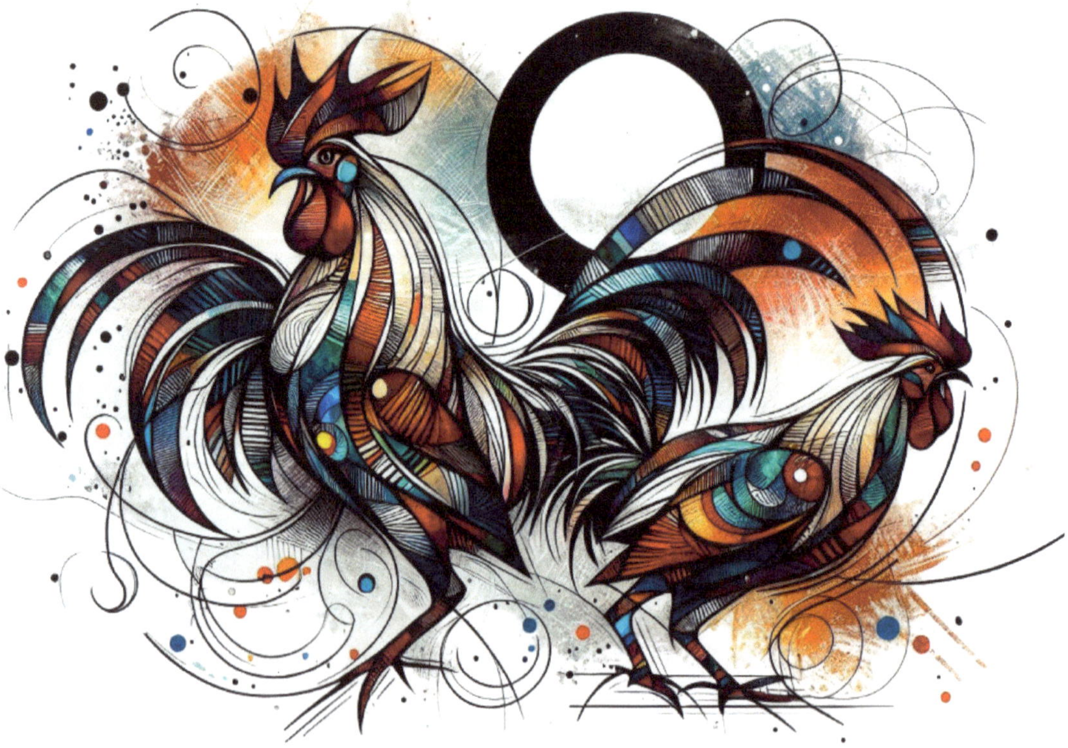

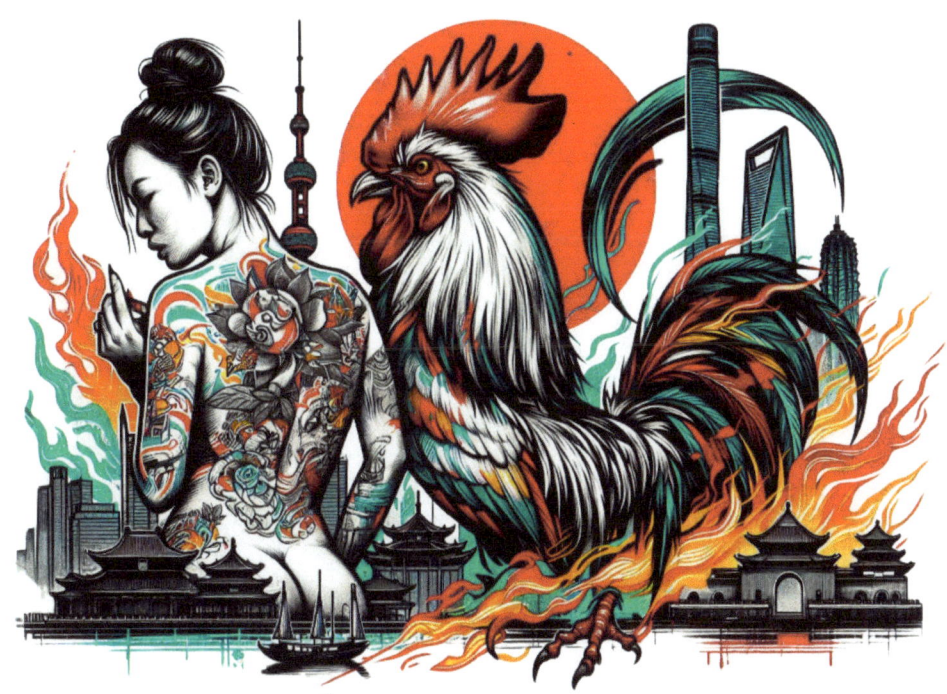

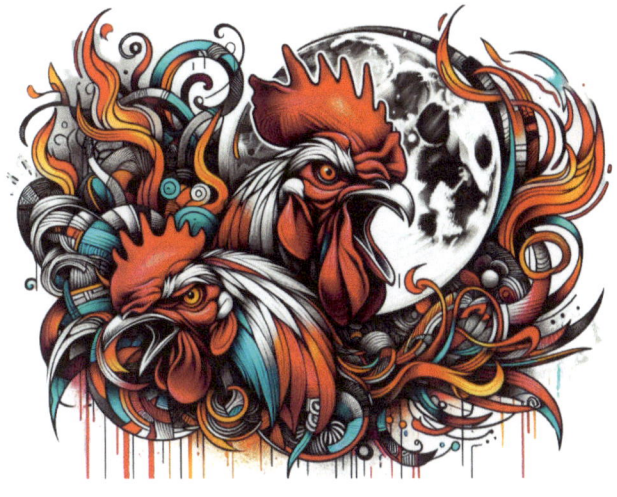

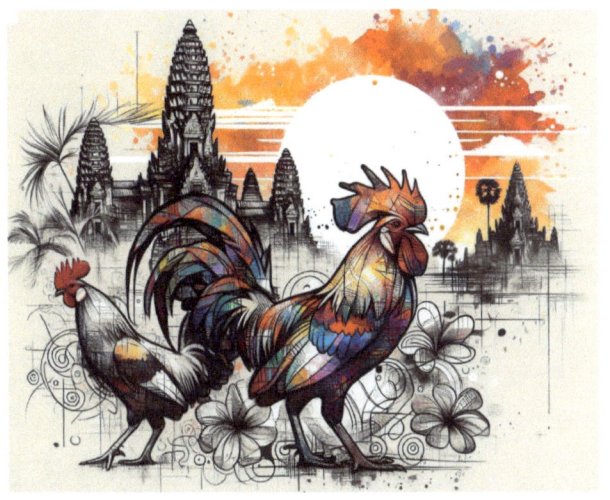

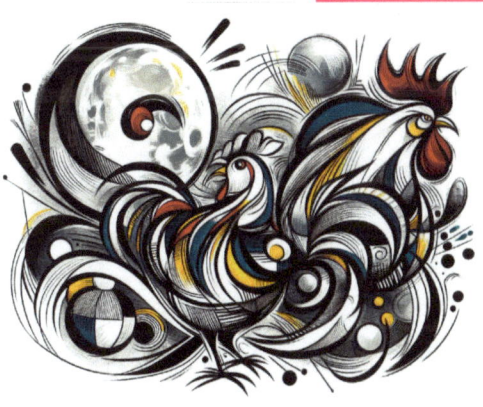

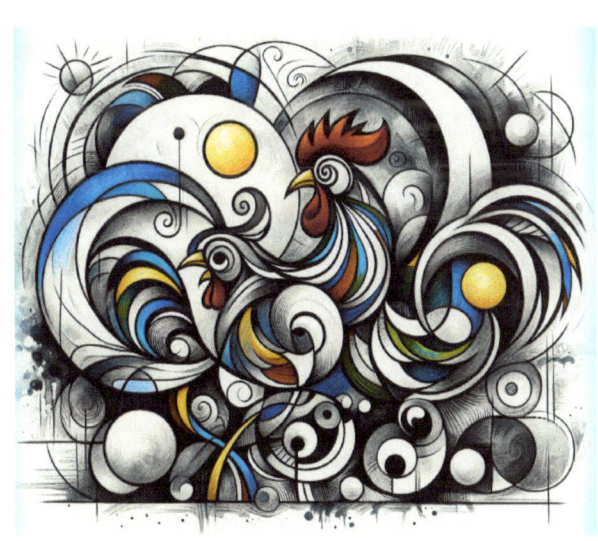

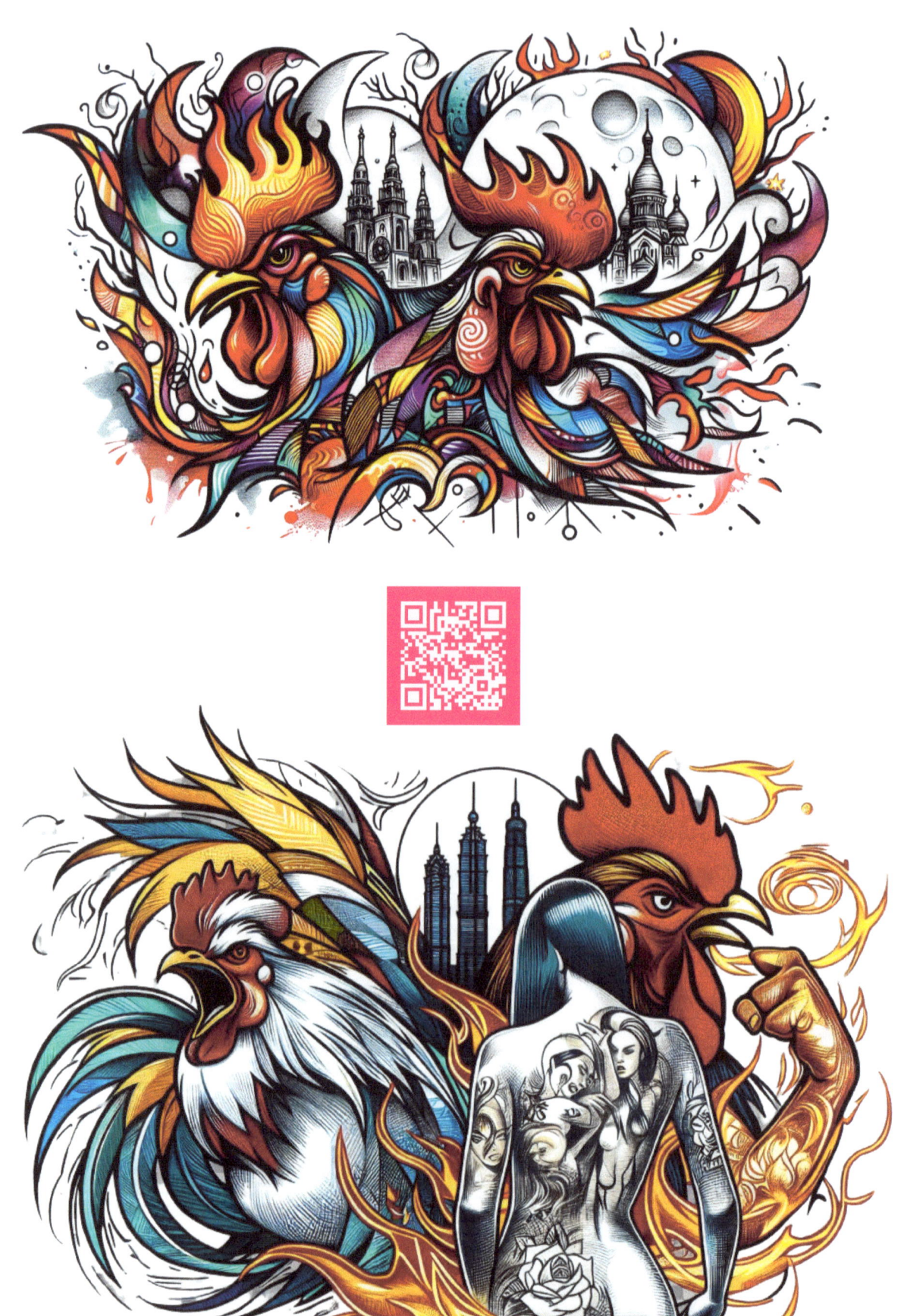

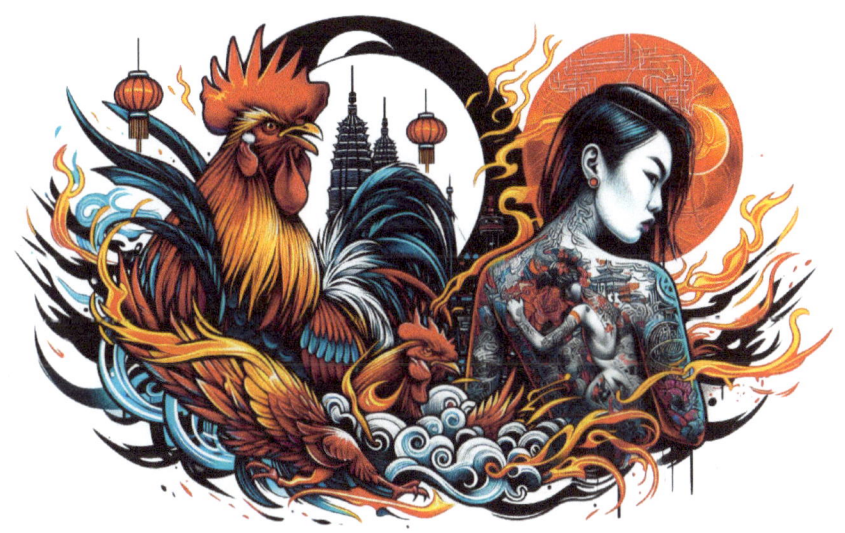

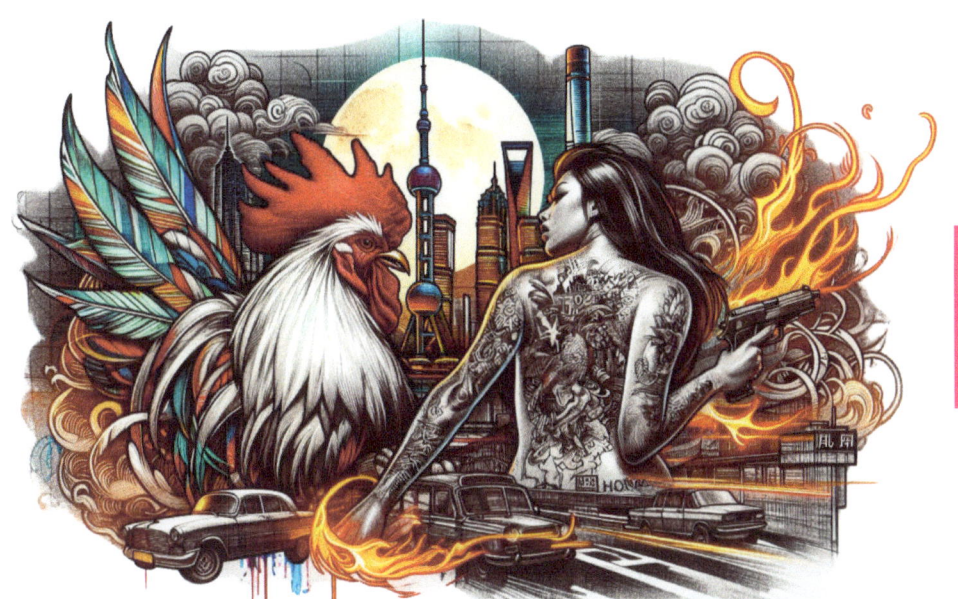

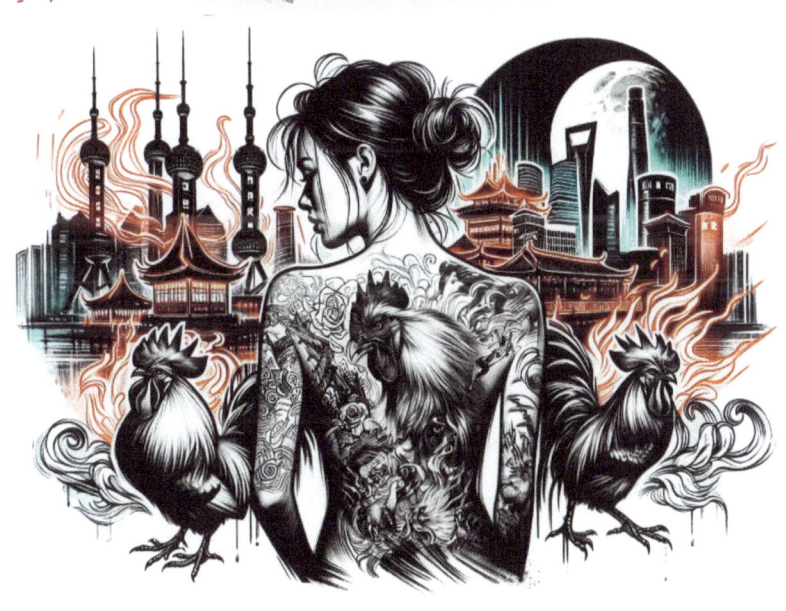

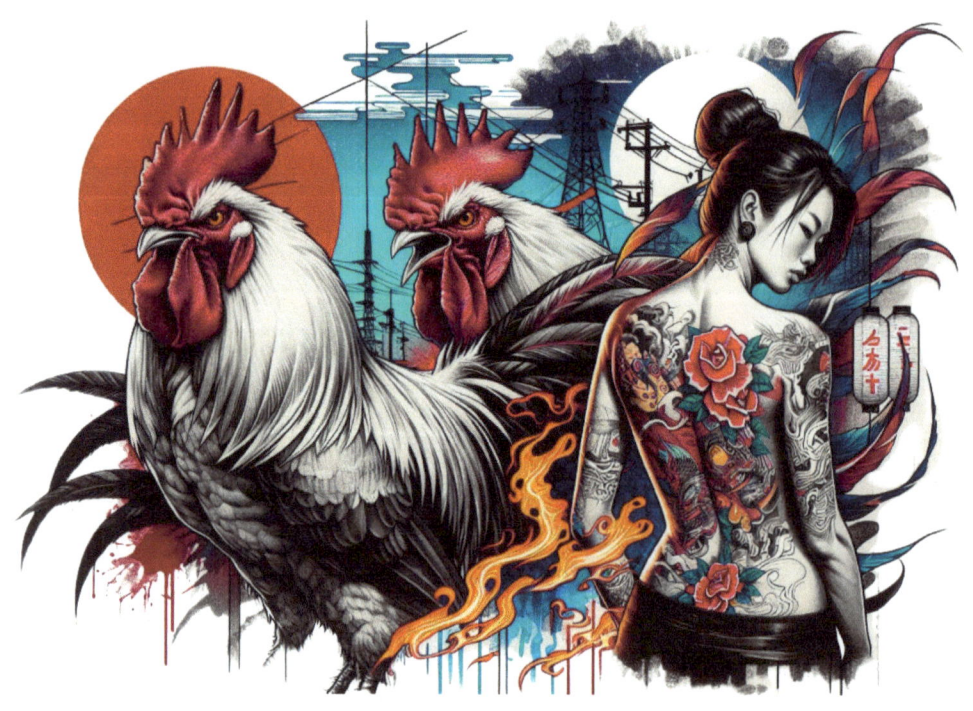

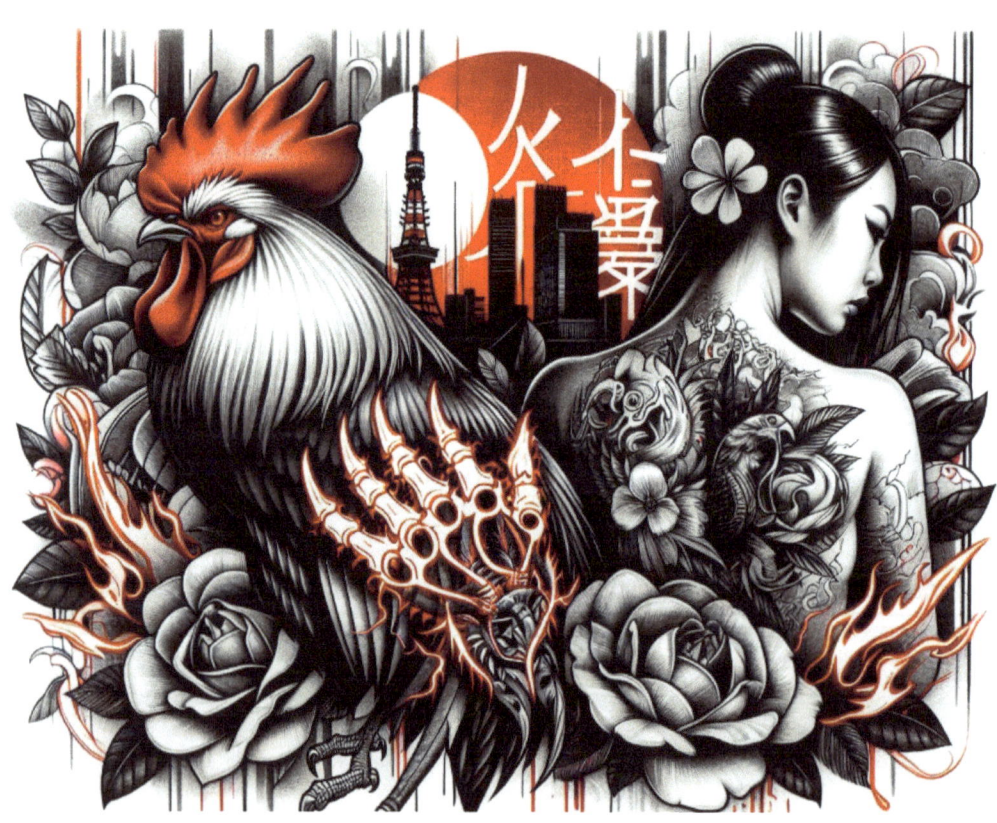

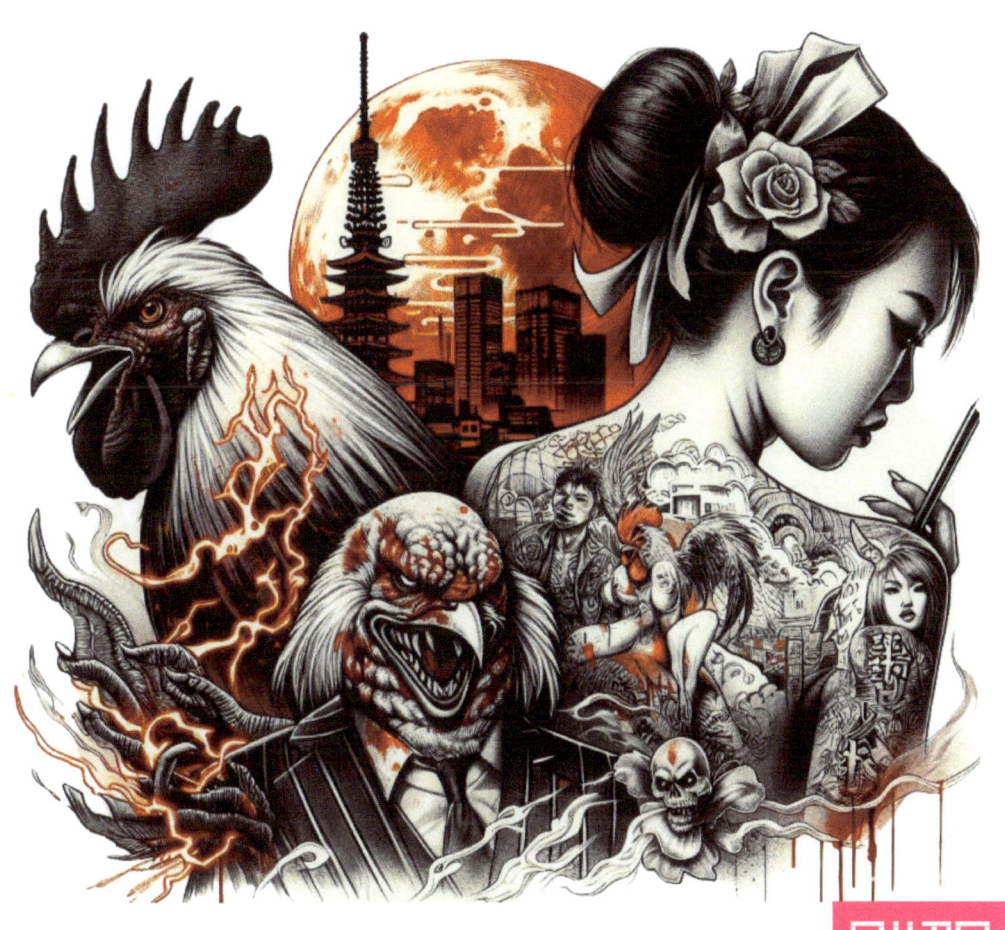

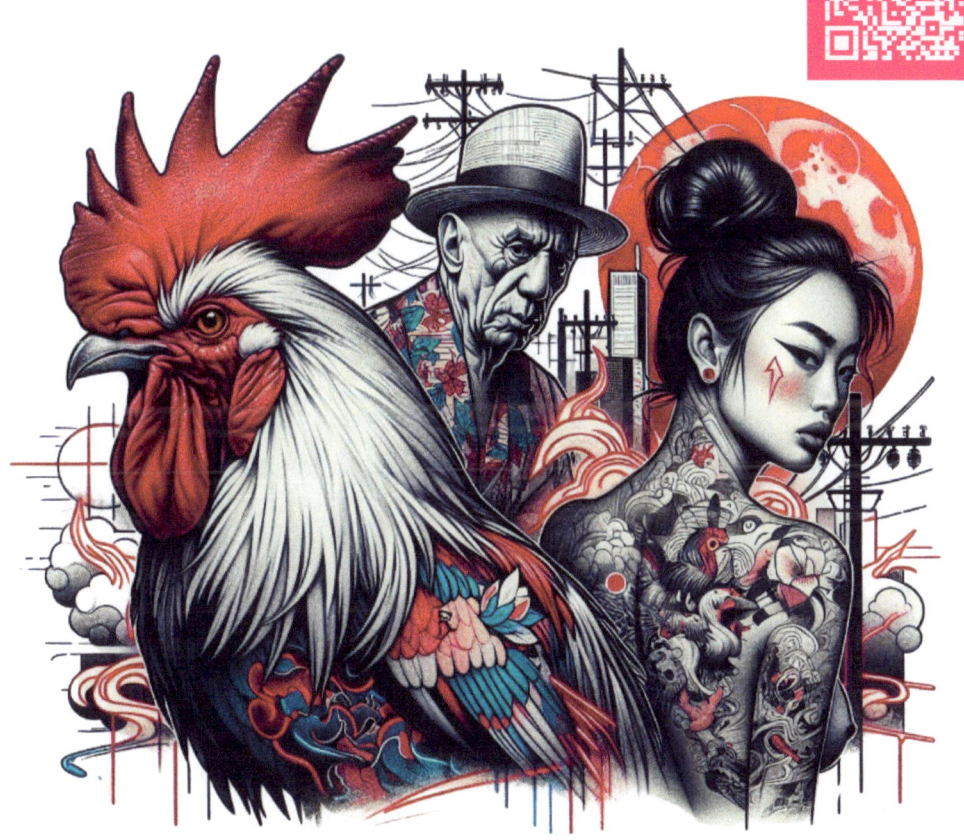

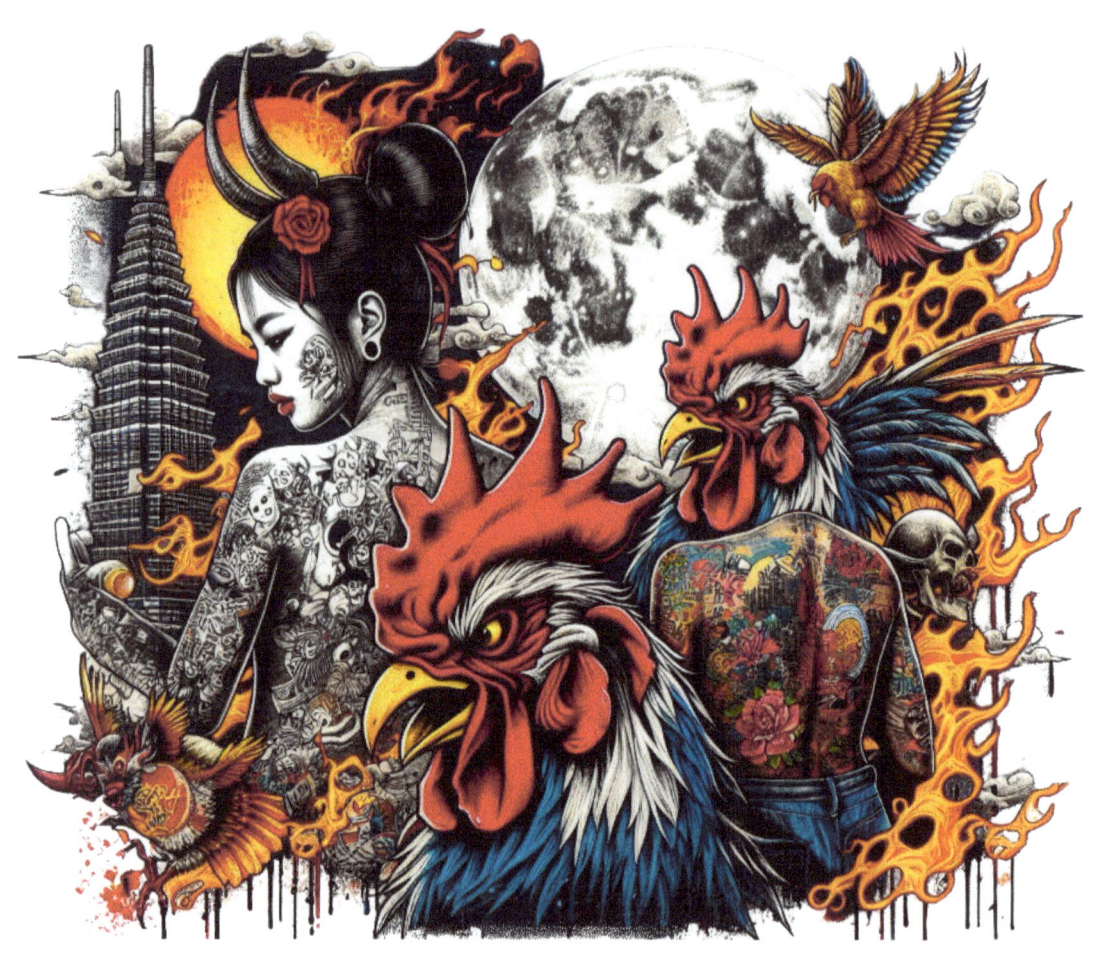

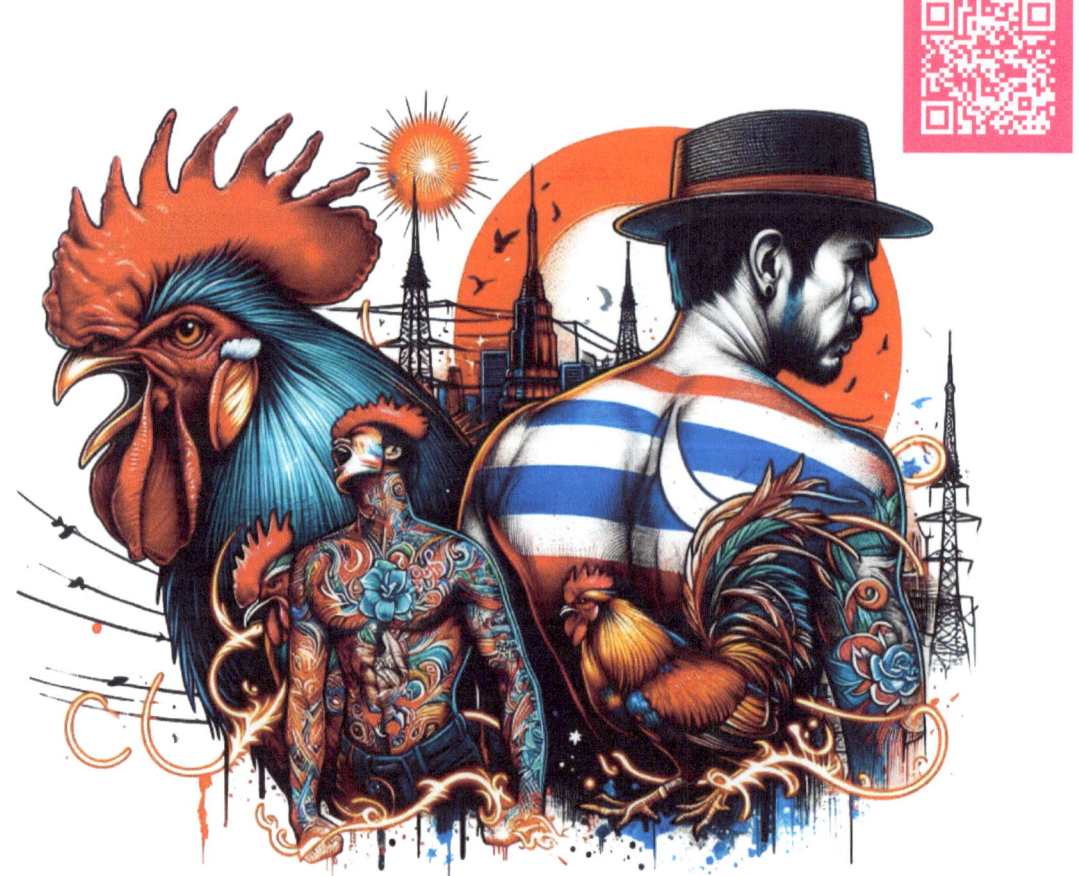

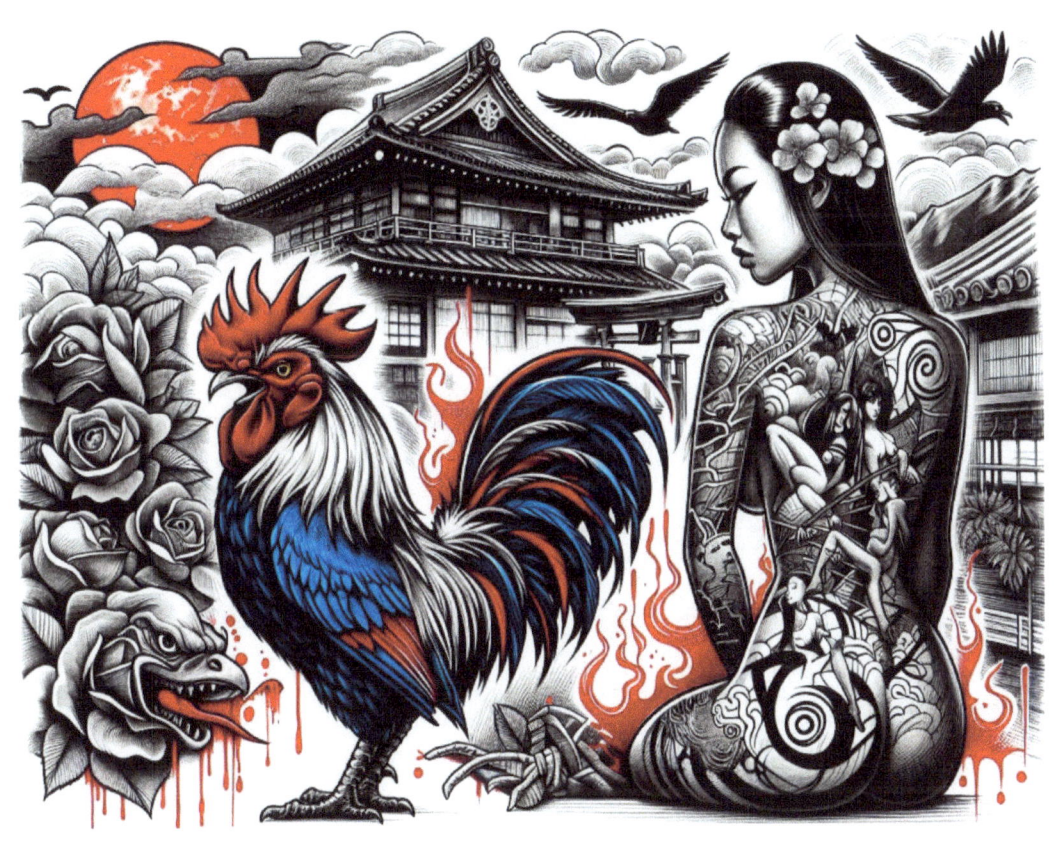

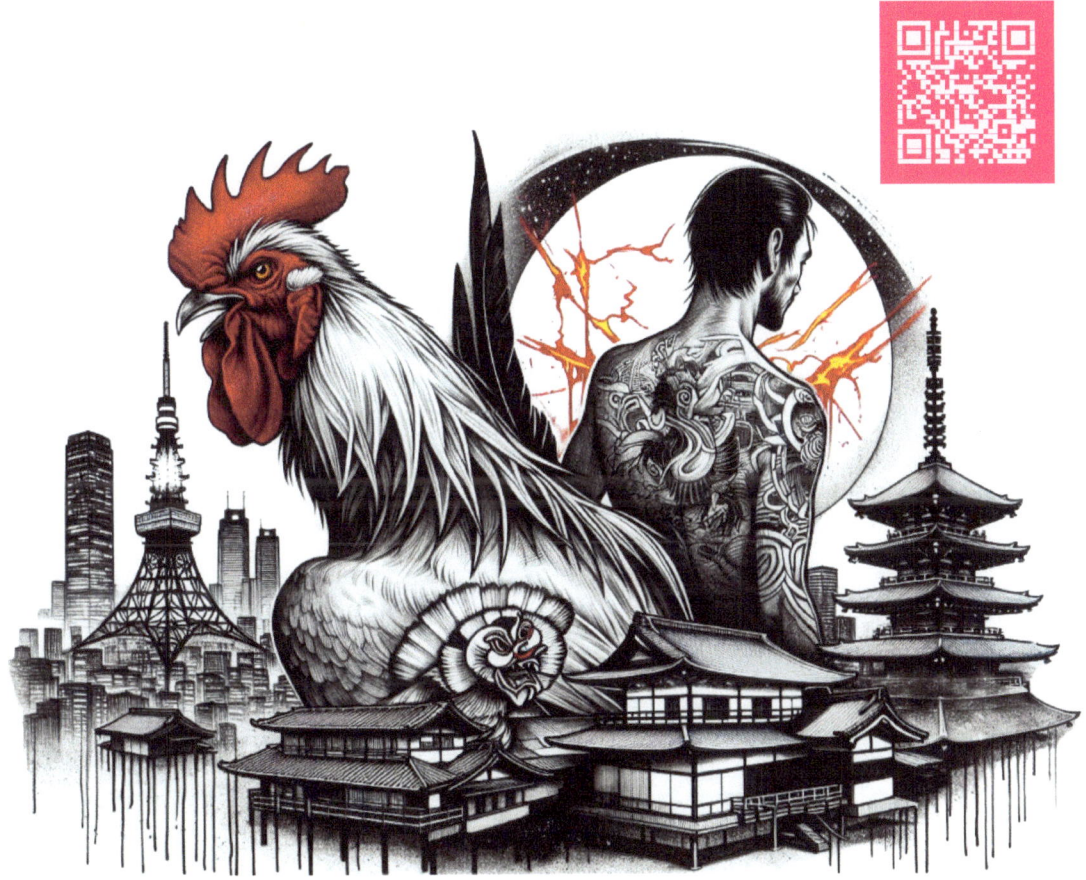

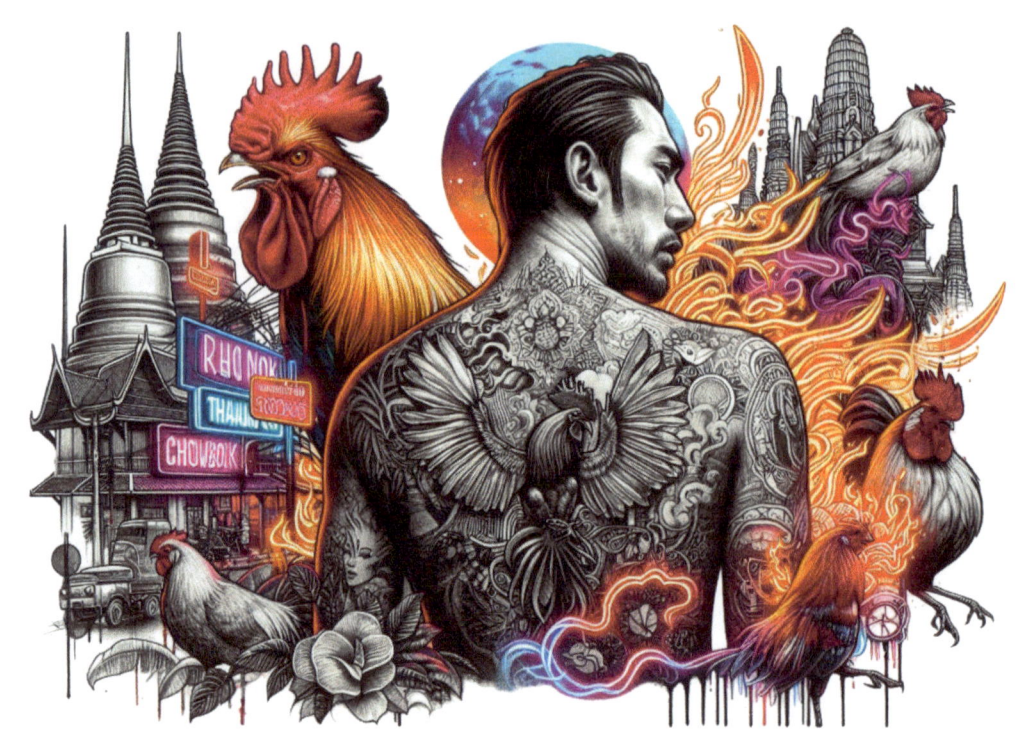

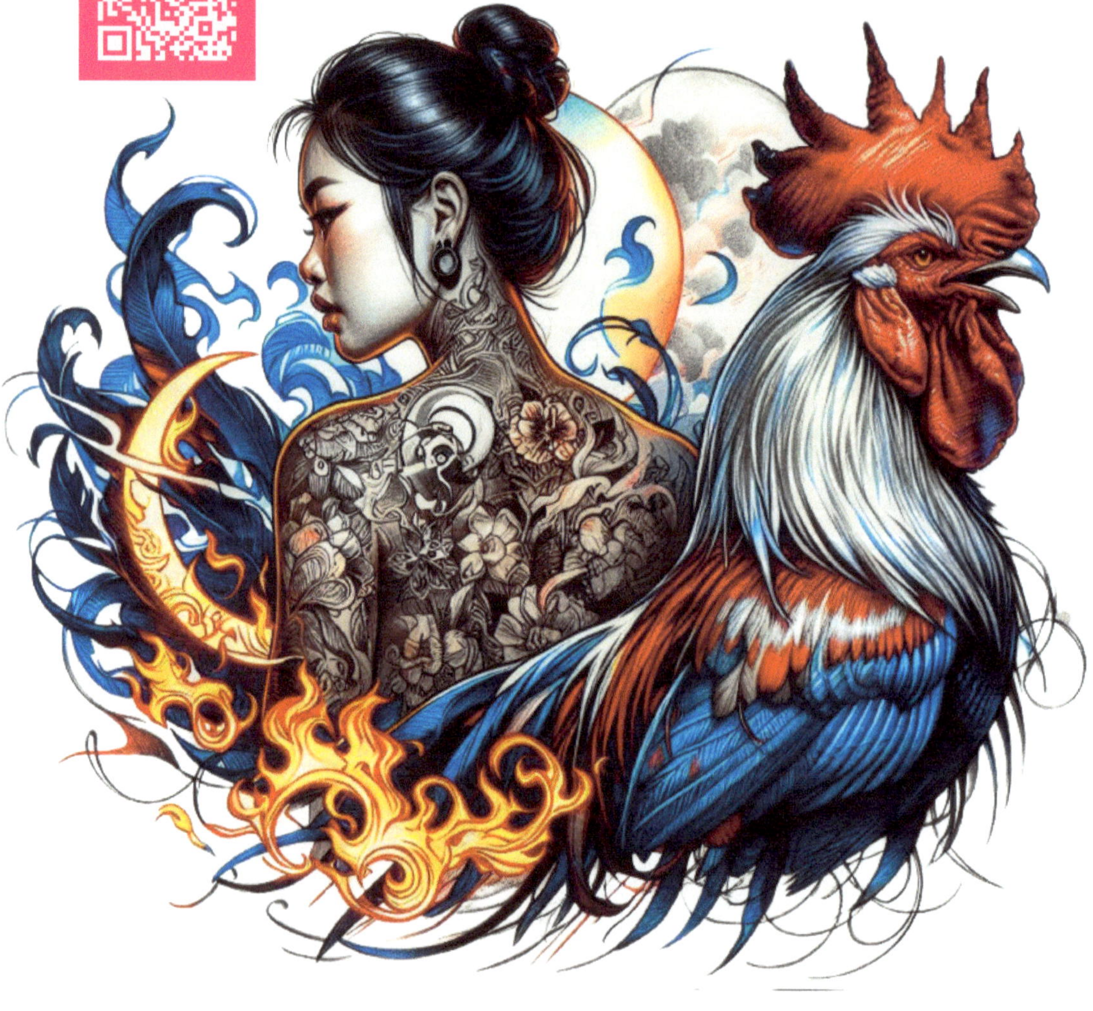

Tiger Section

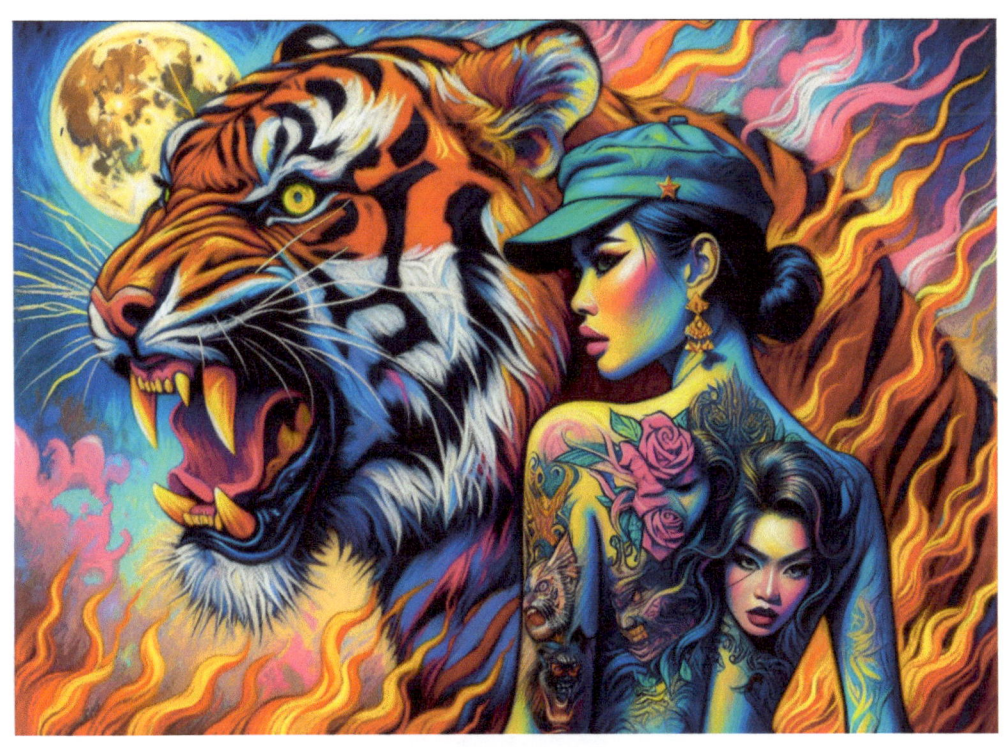

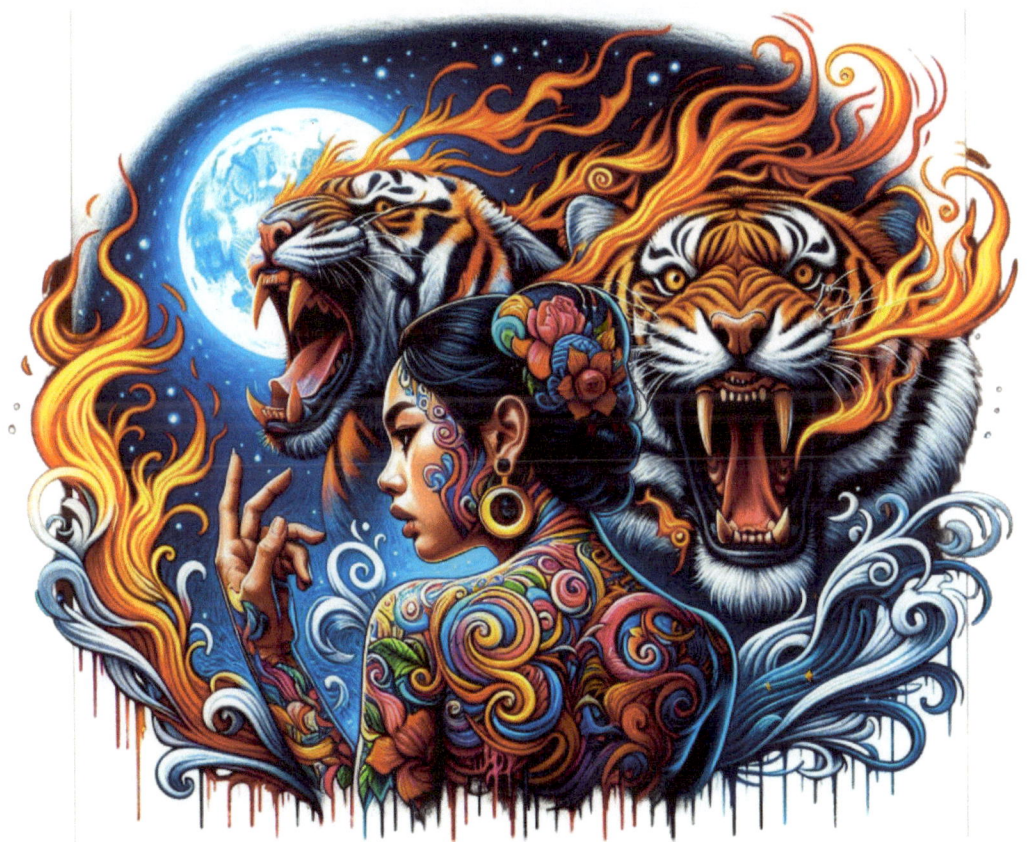

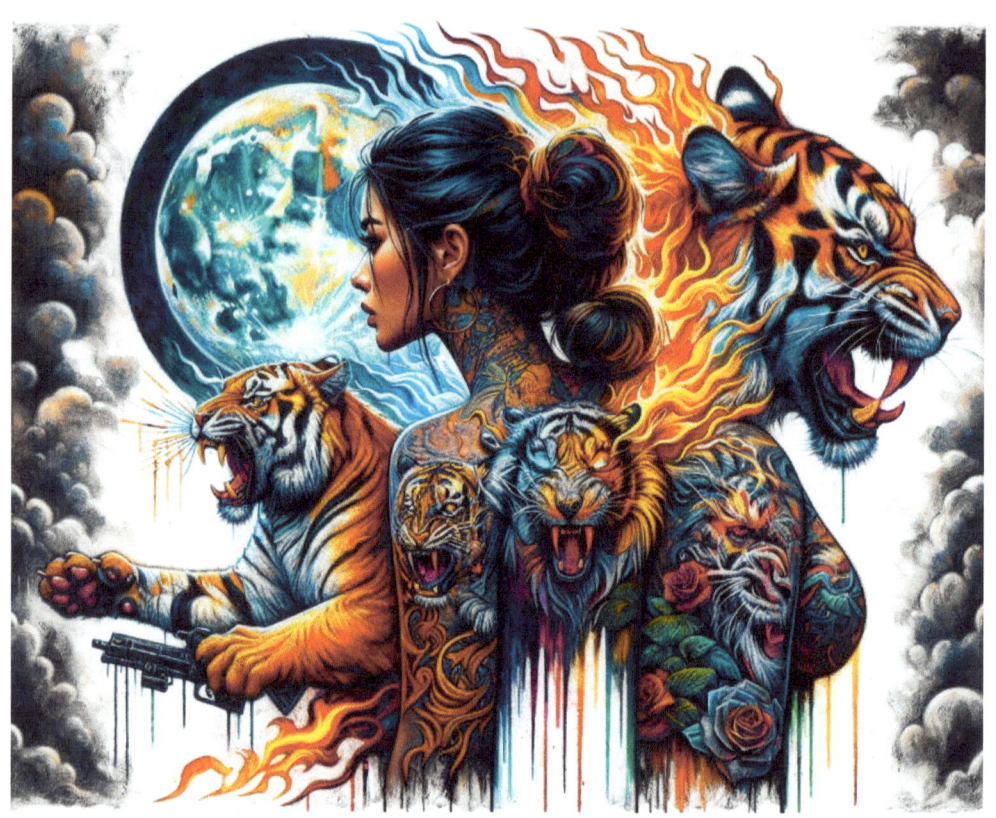

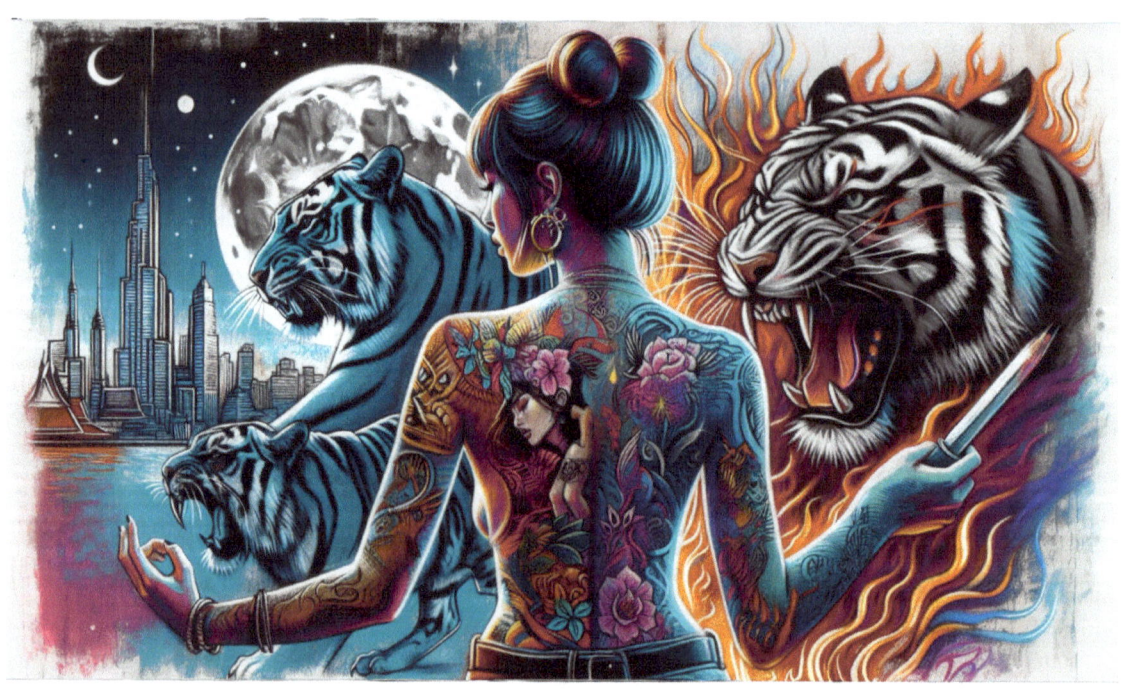

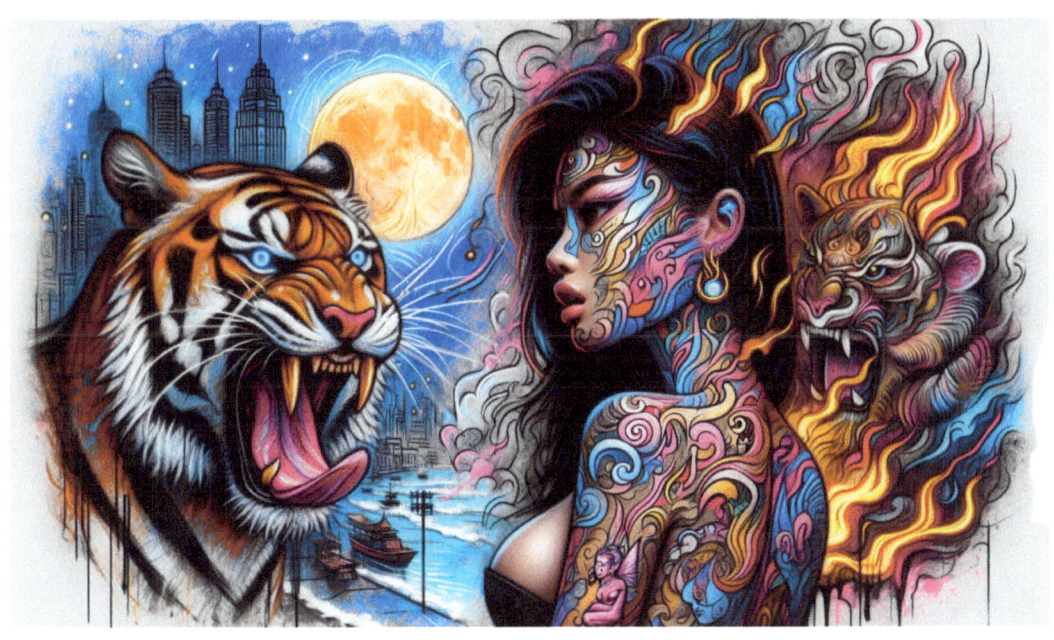

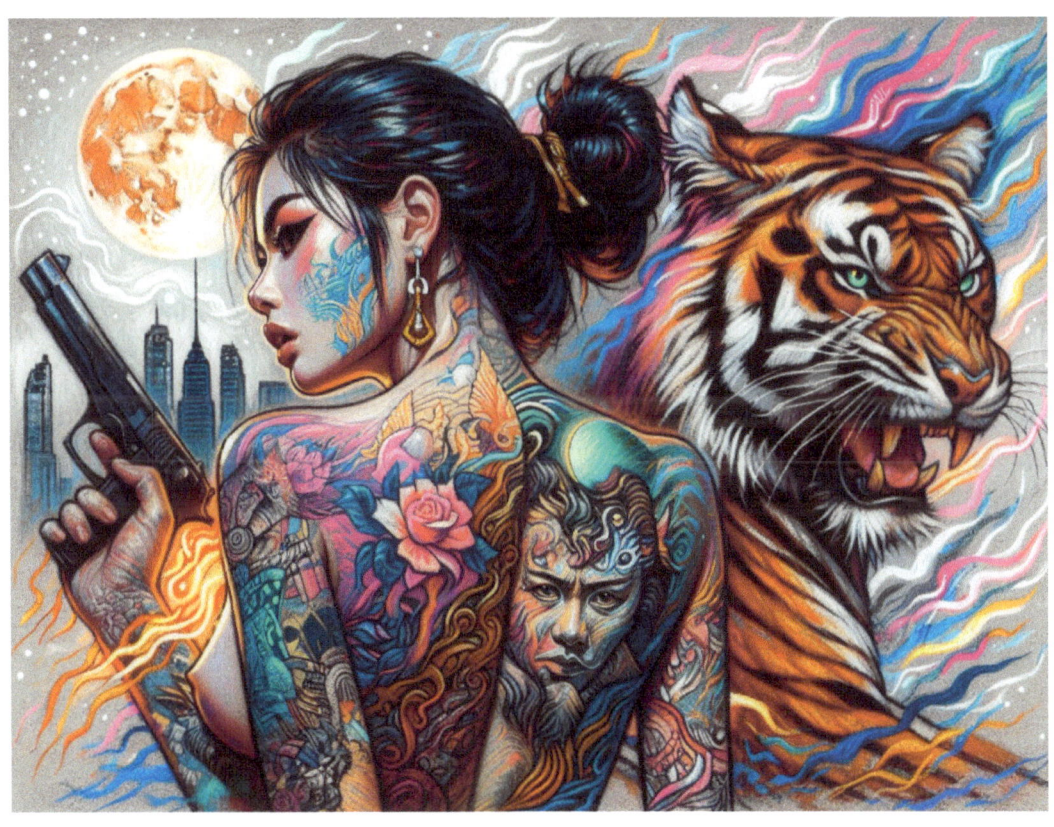

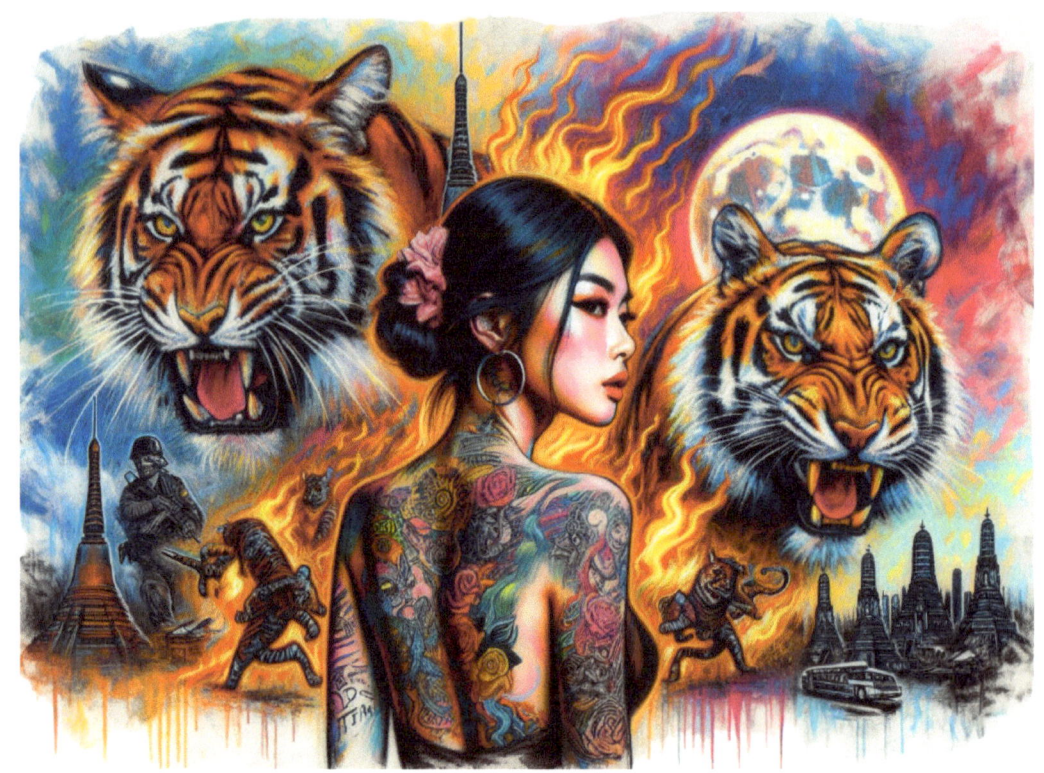

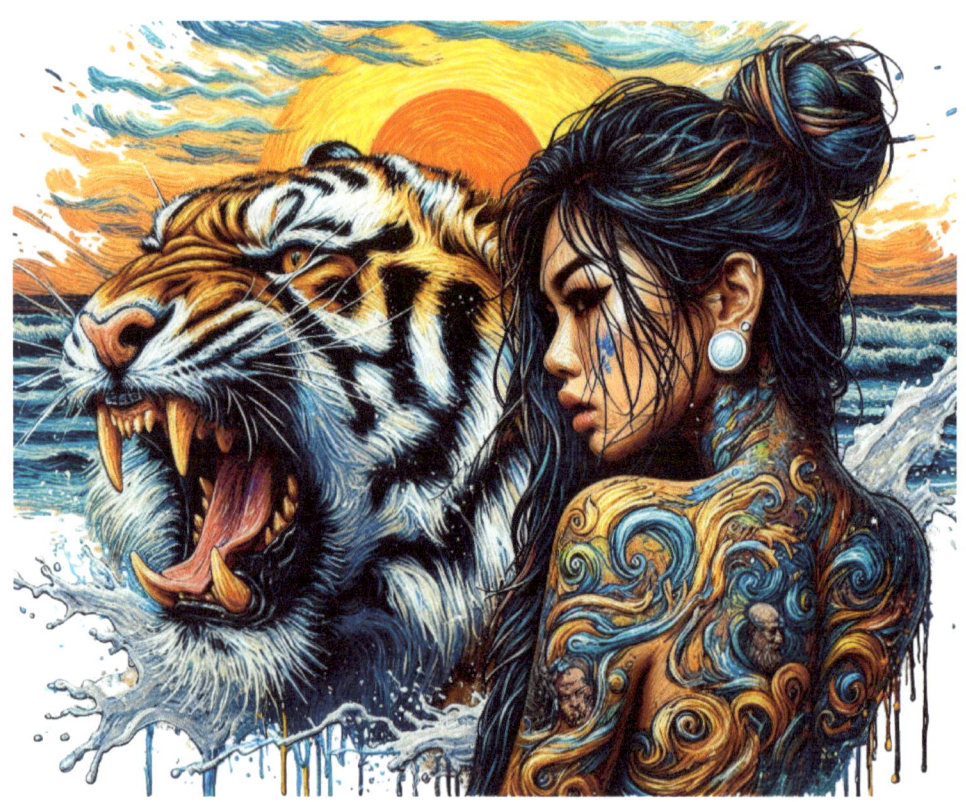

Serpent Section

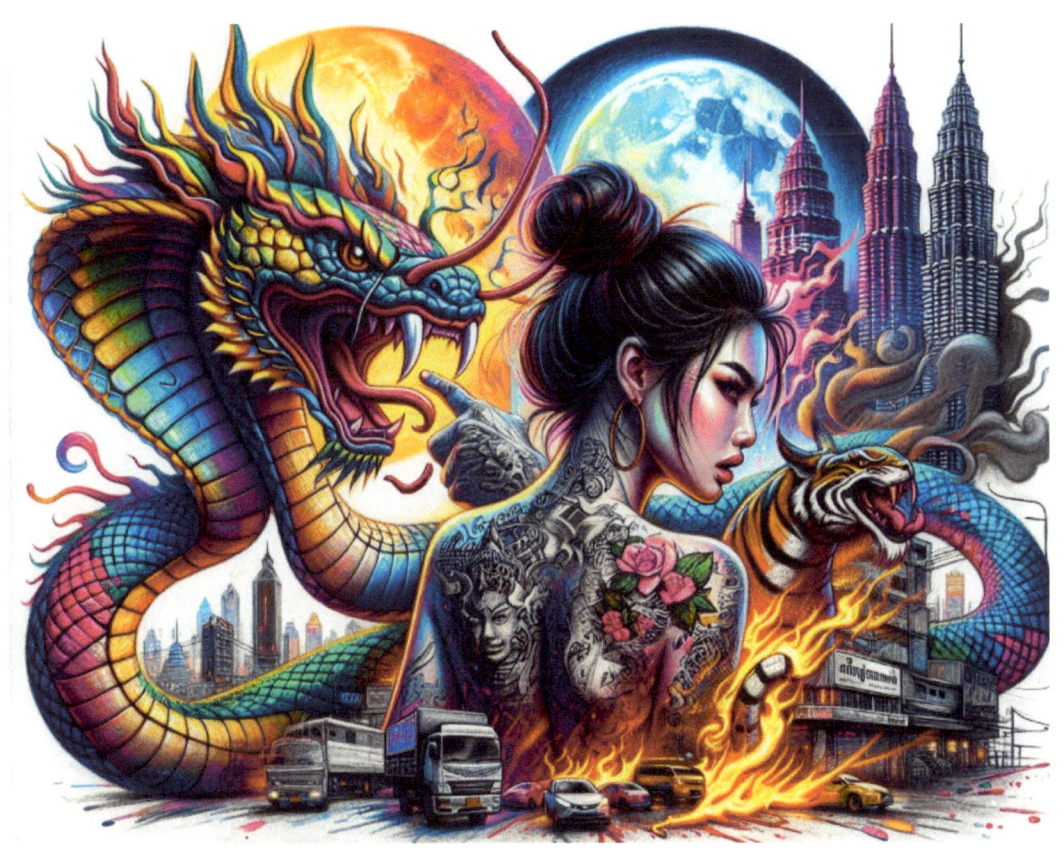

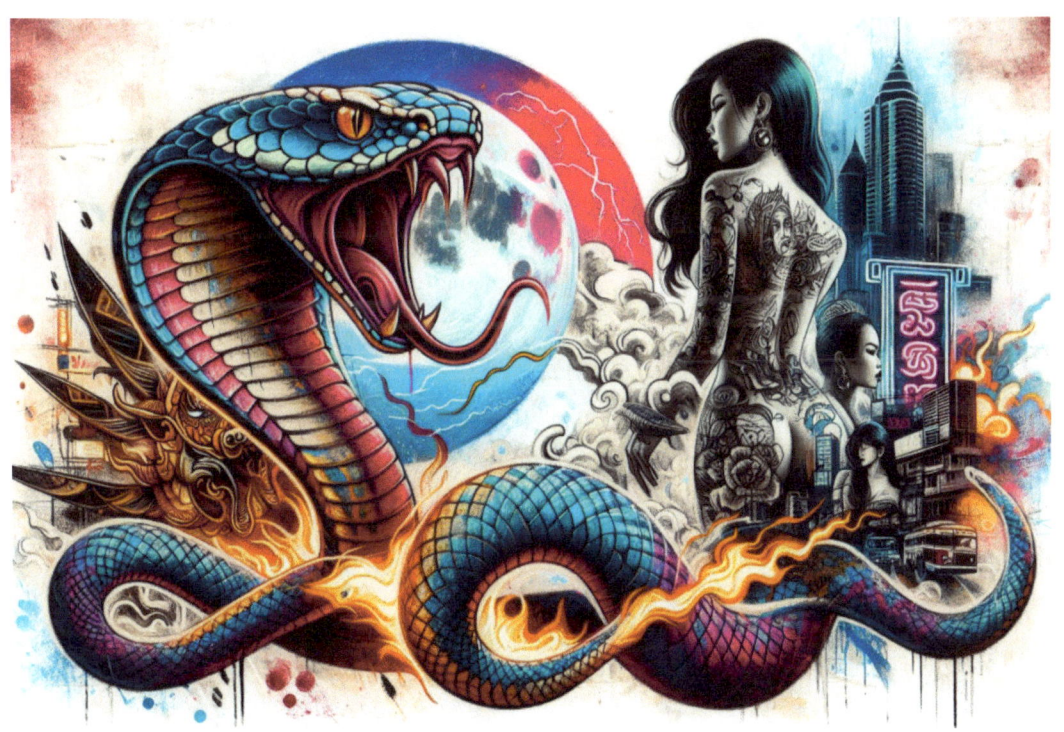

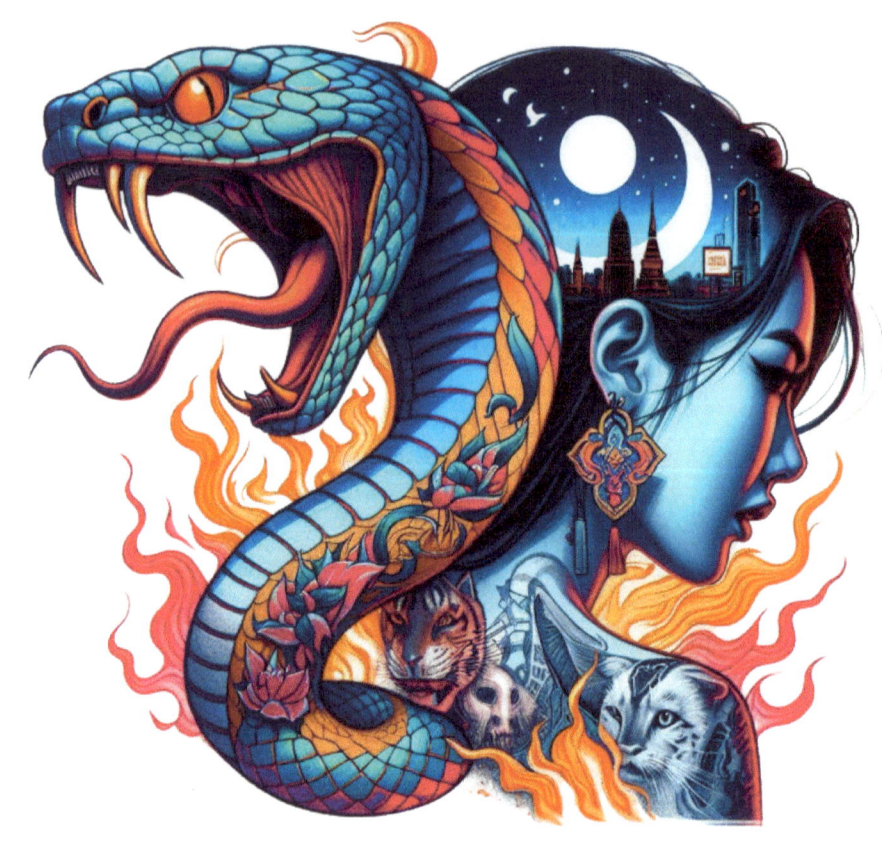

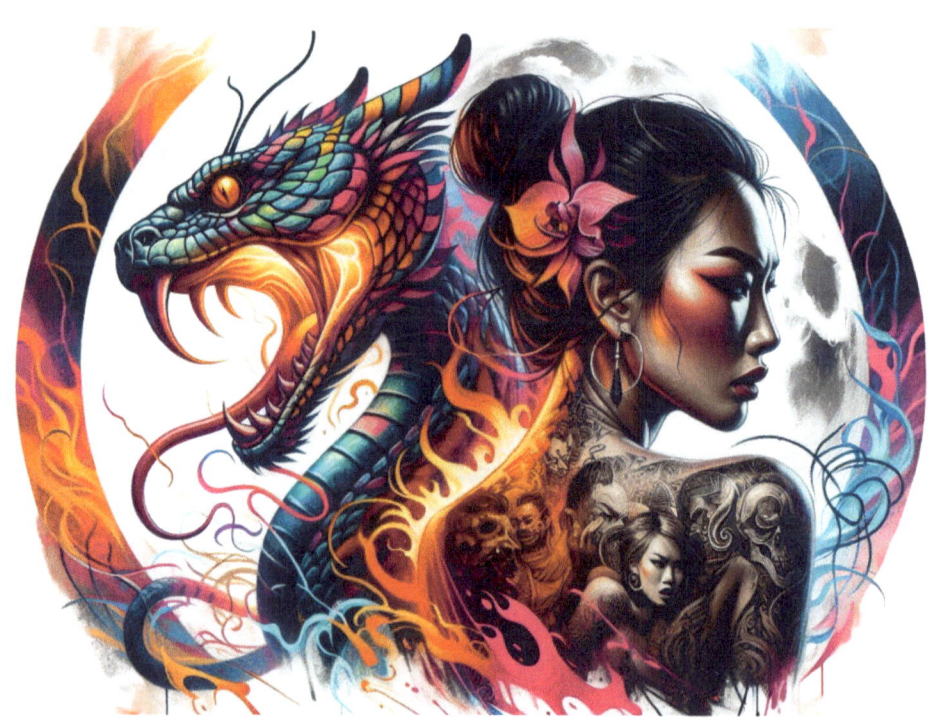

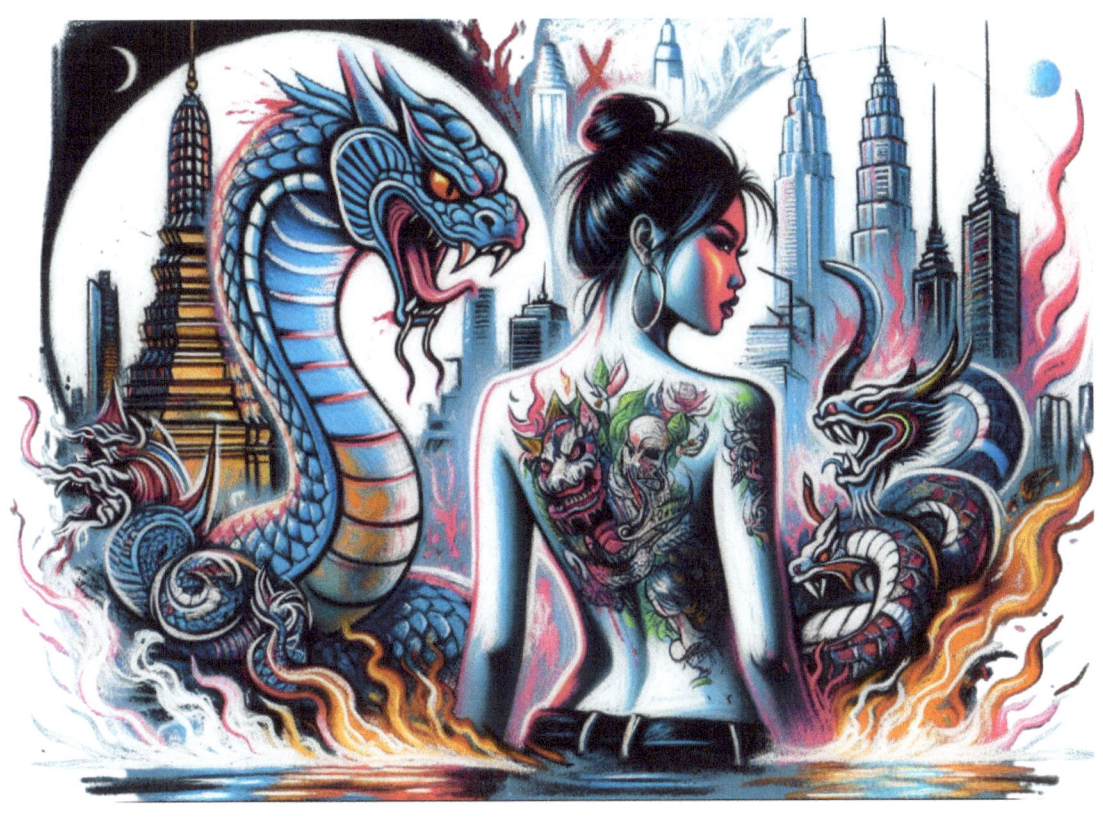

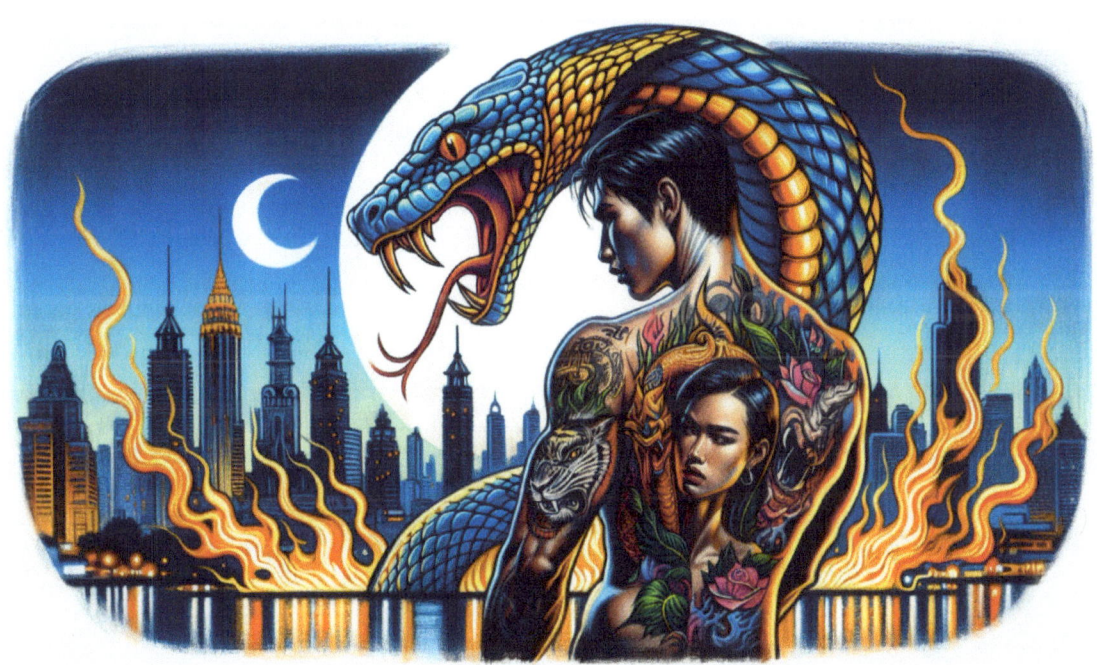

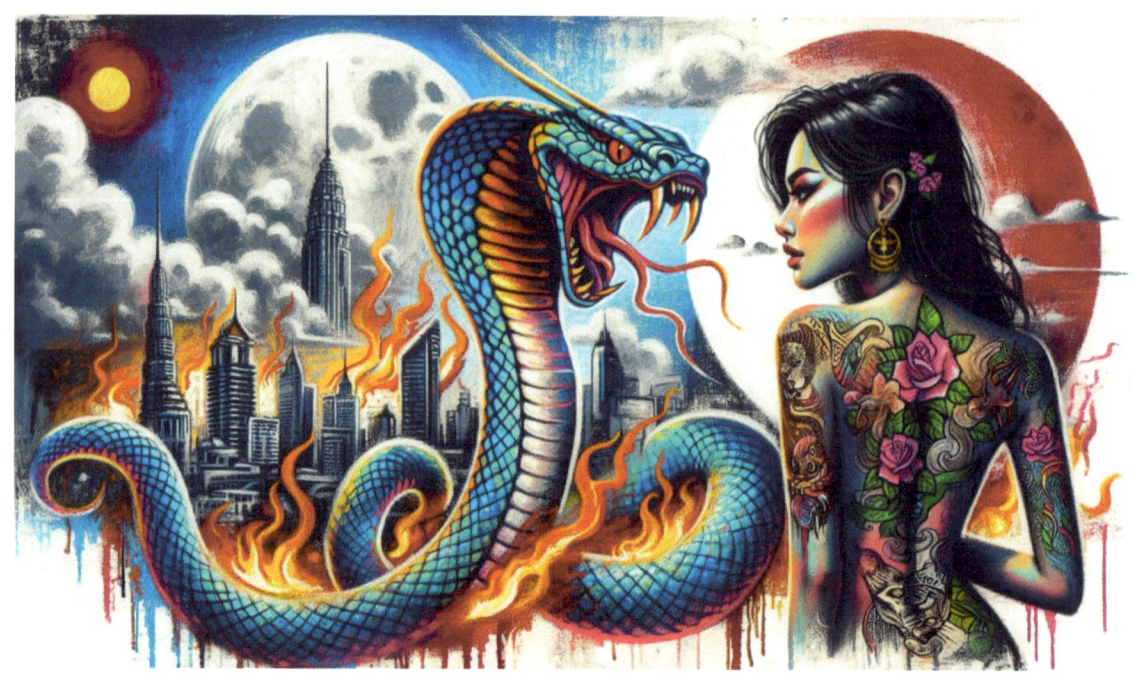

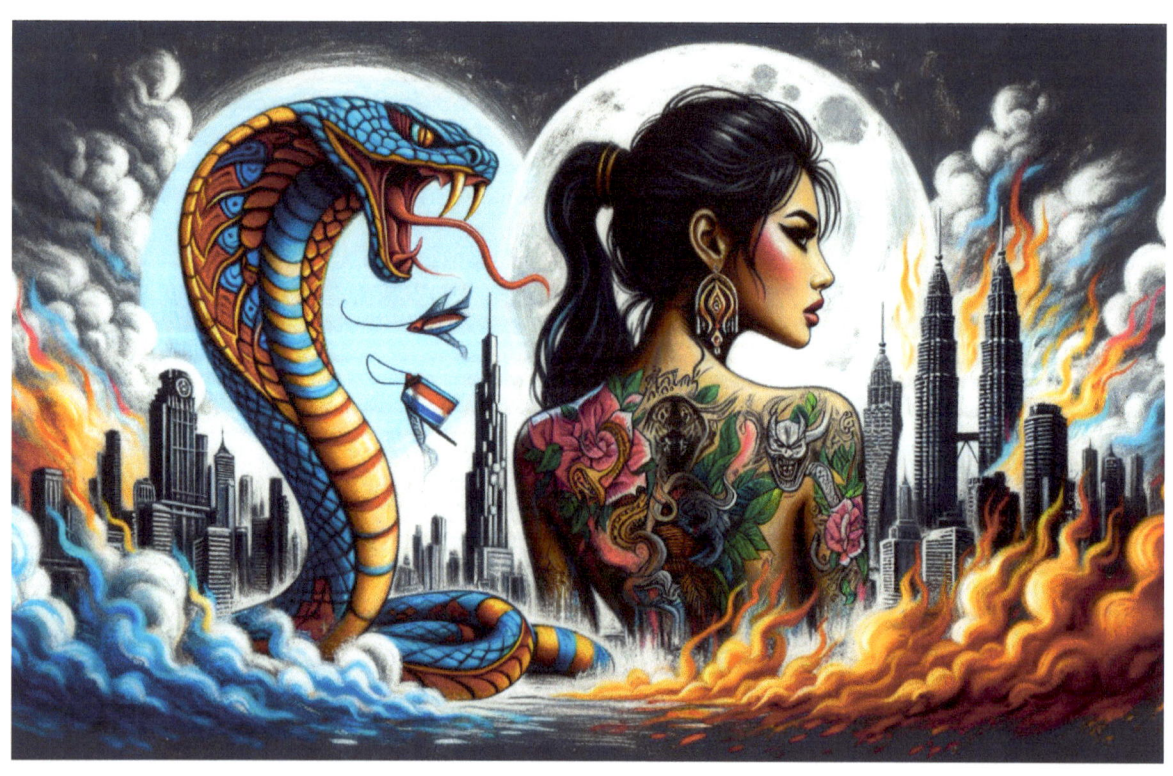

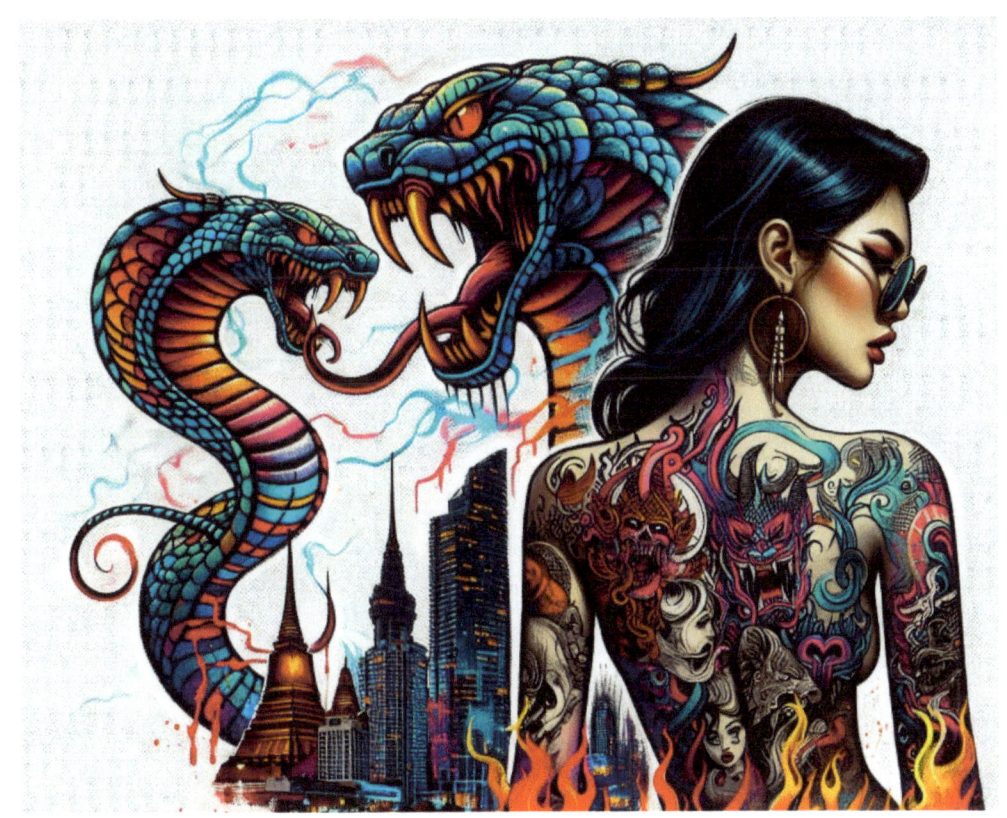

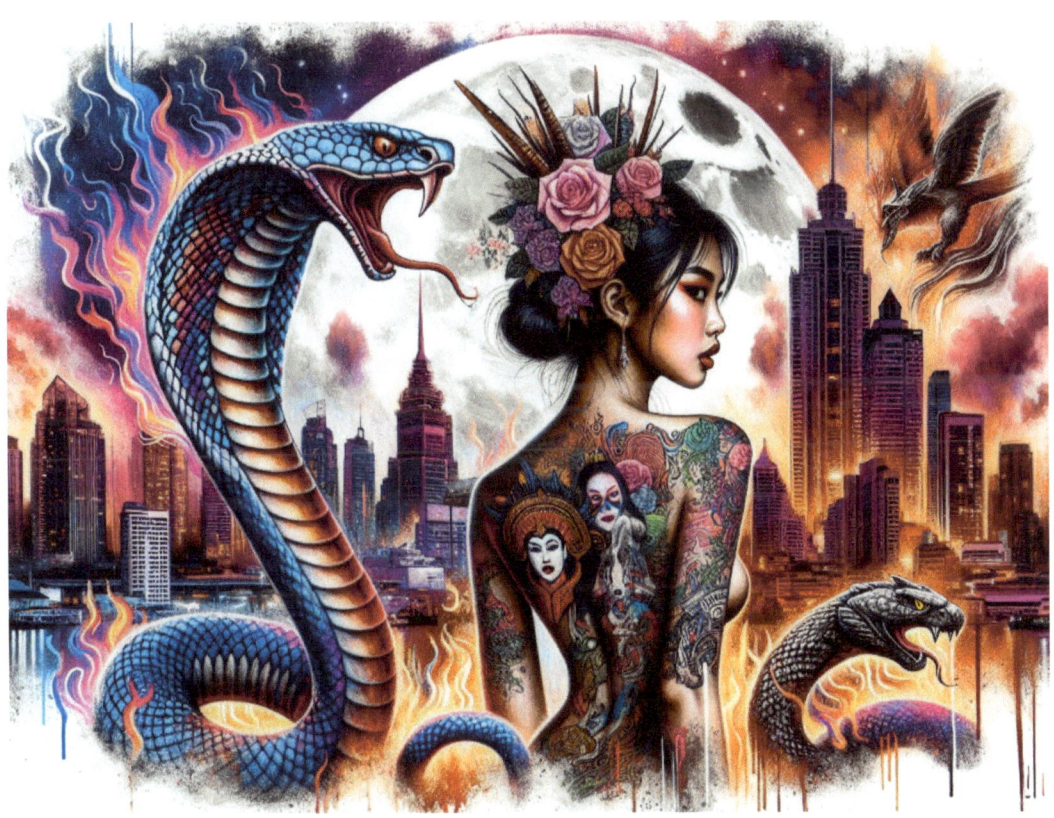

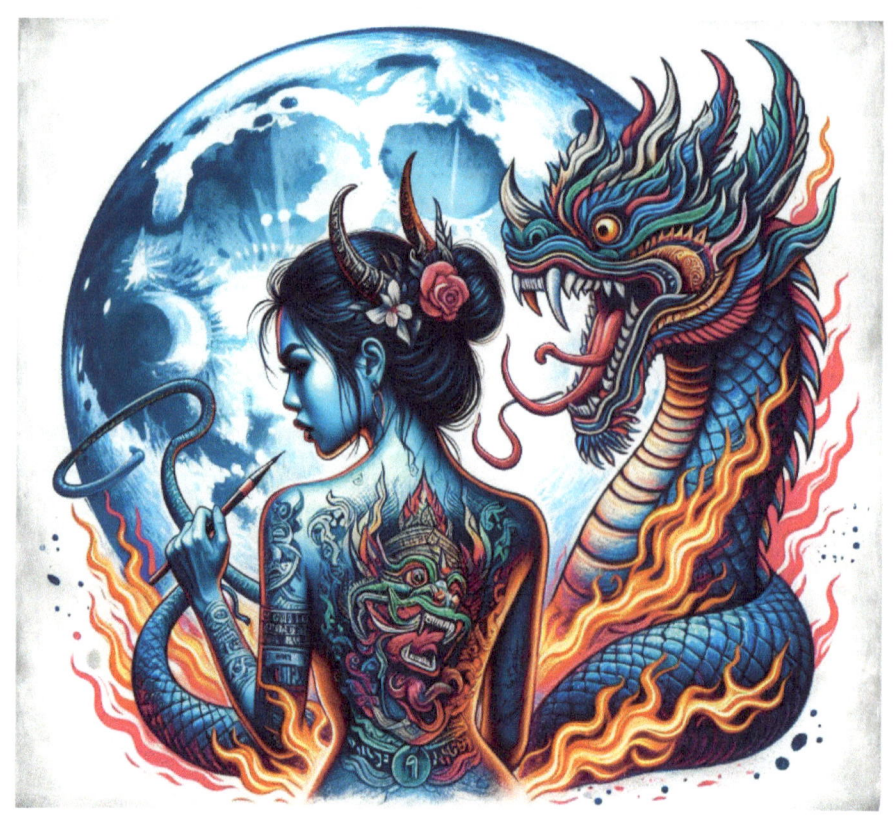

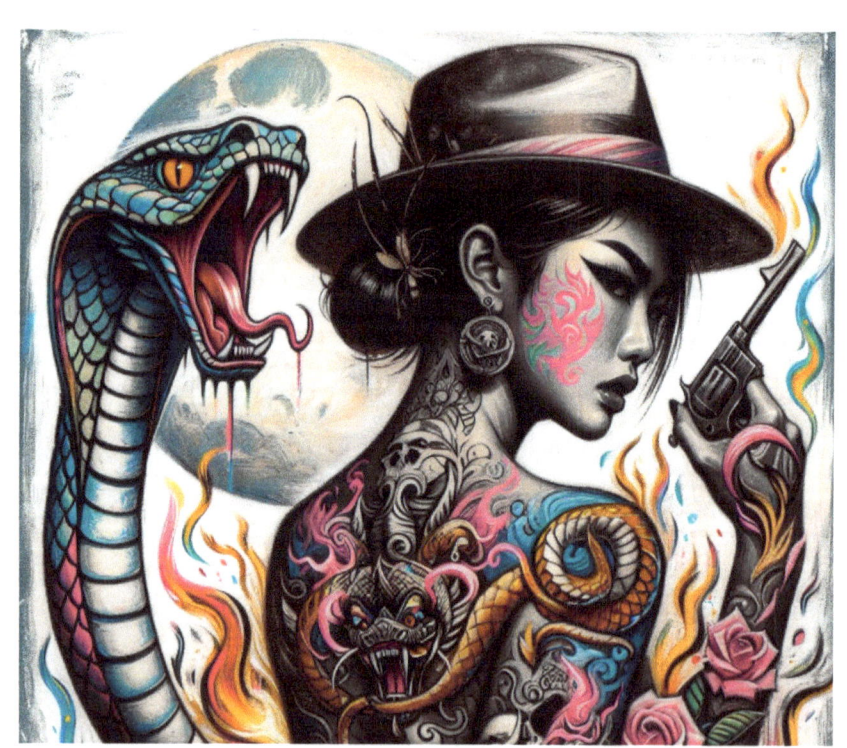

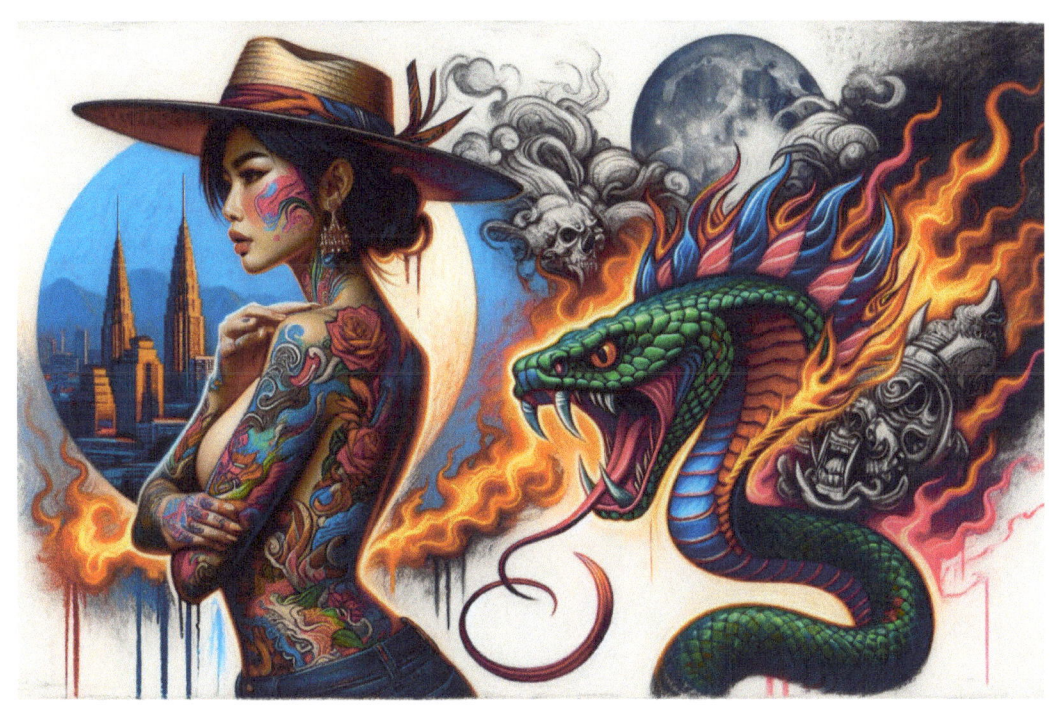

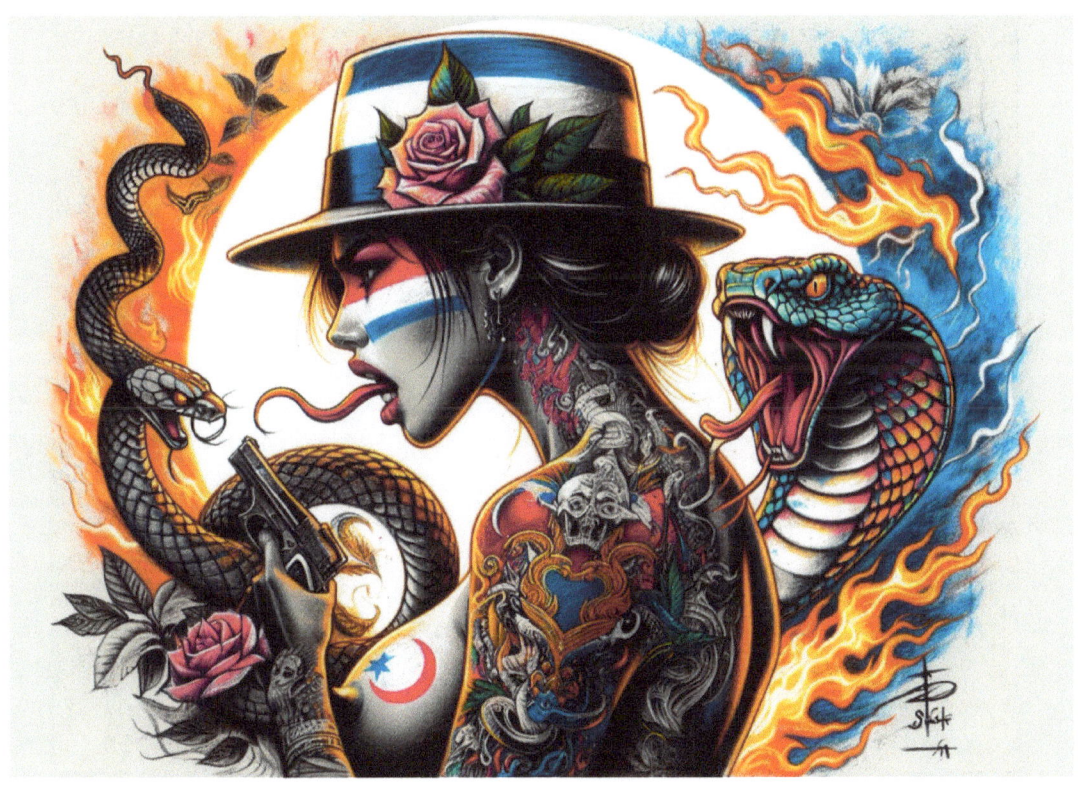

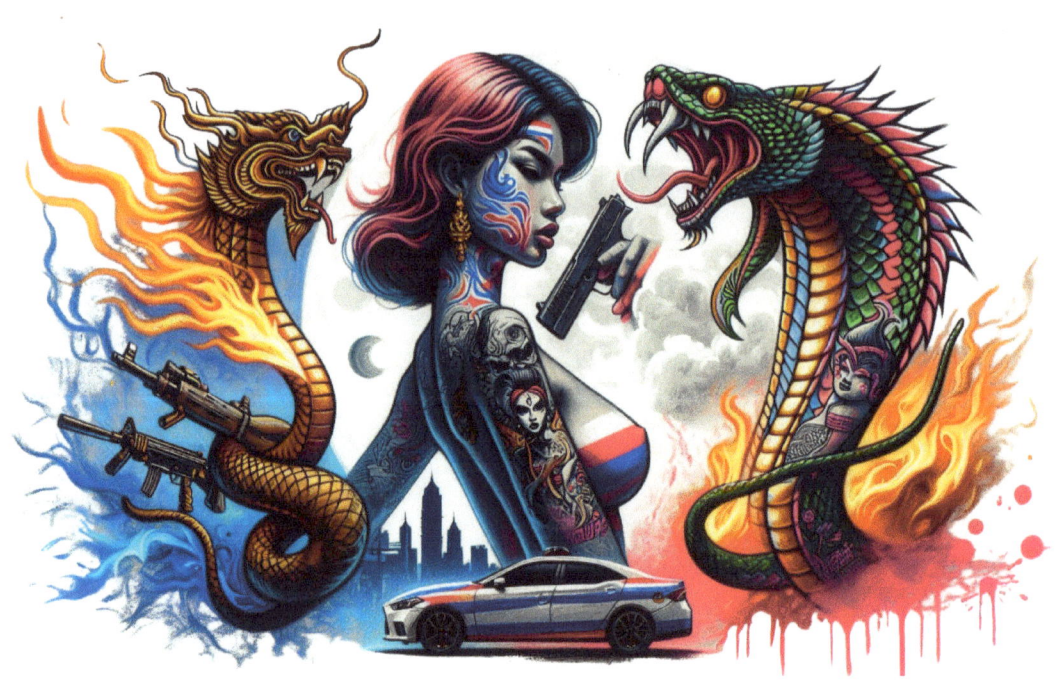

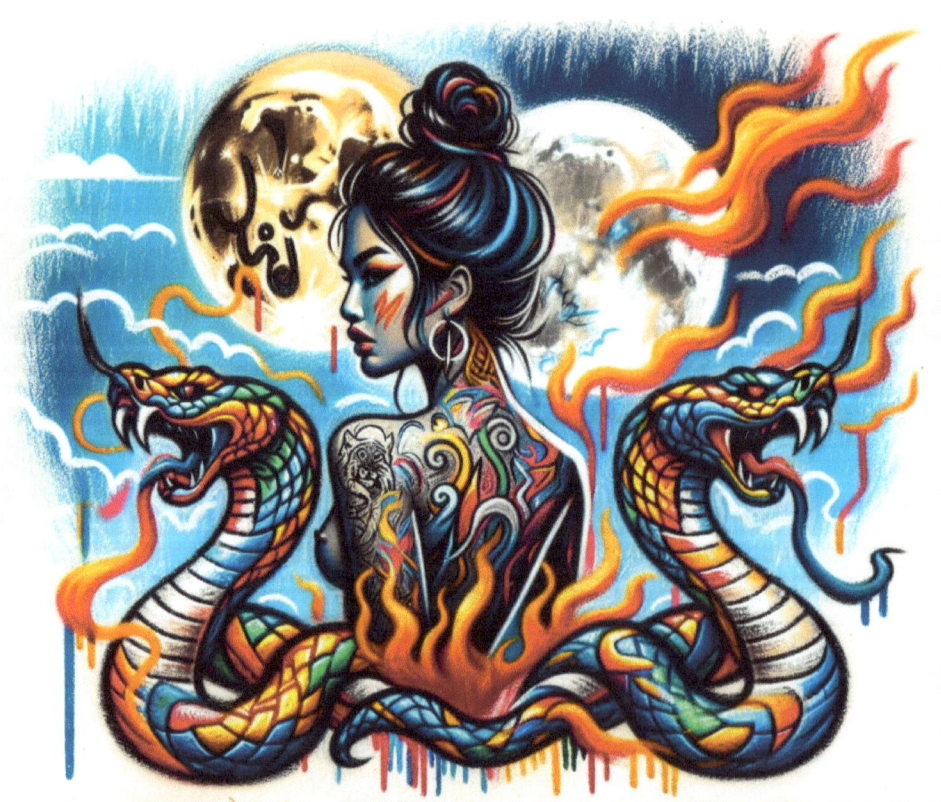

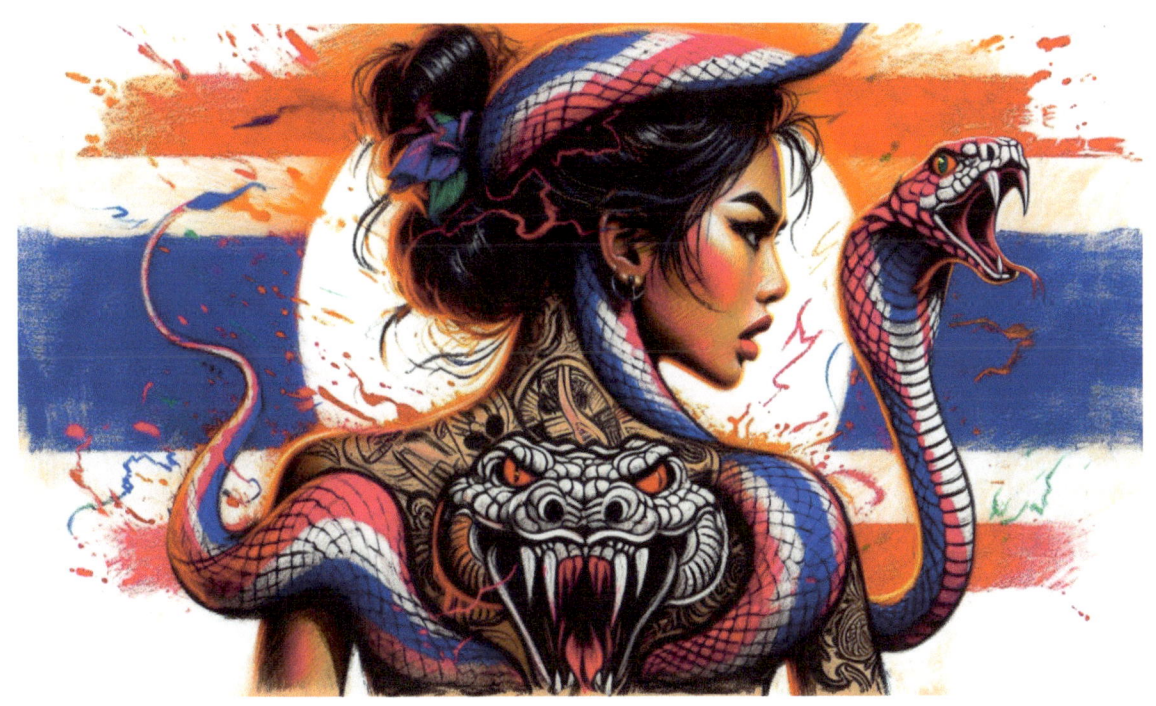

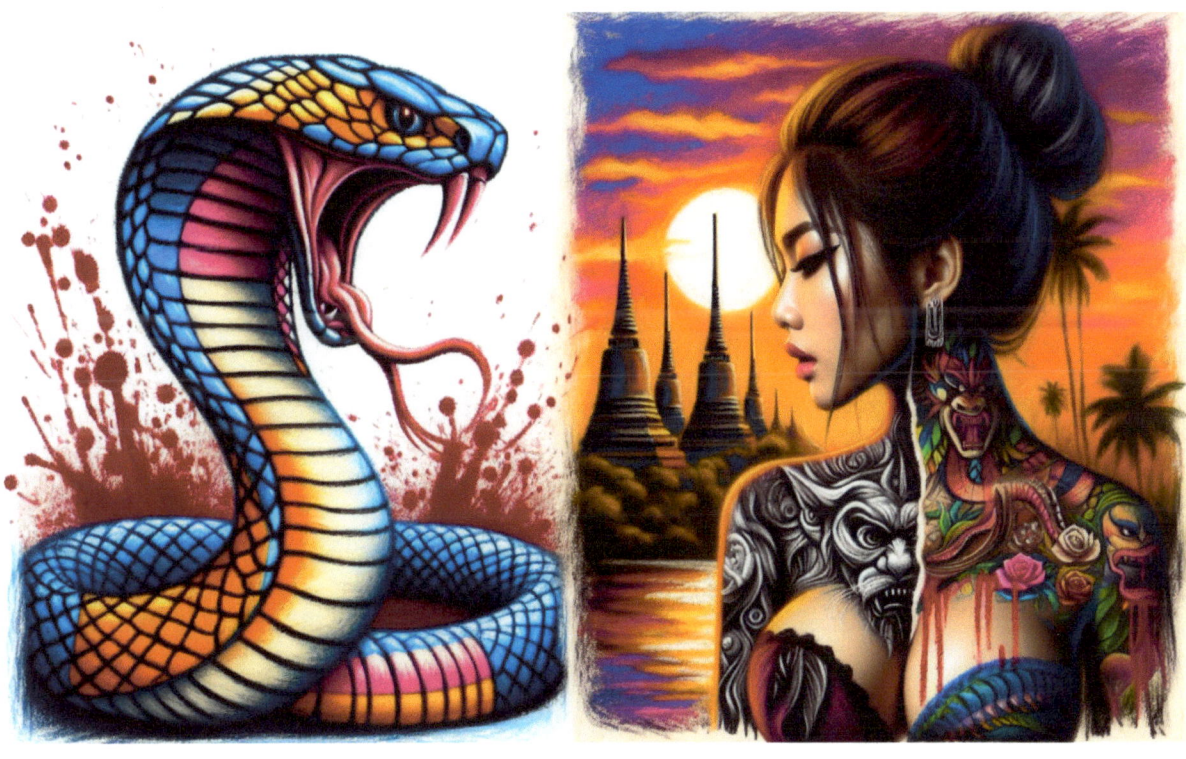

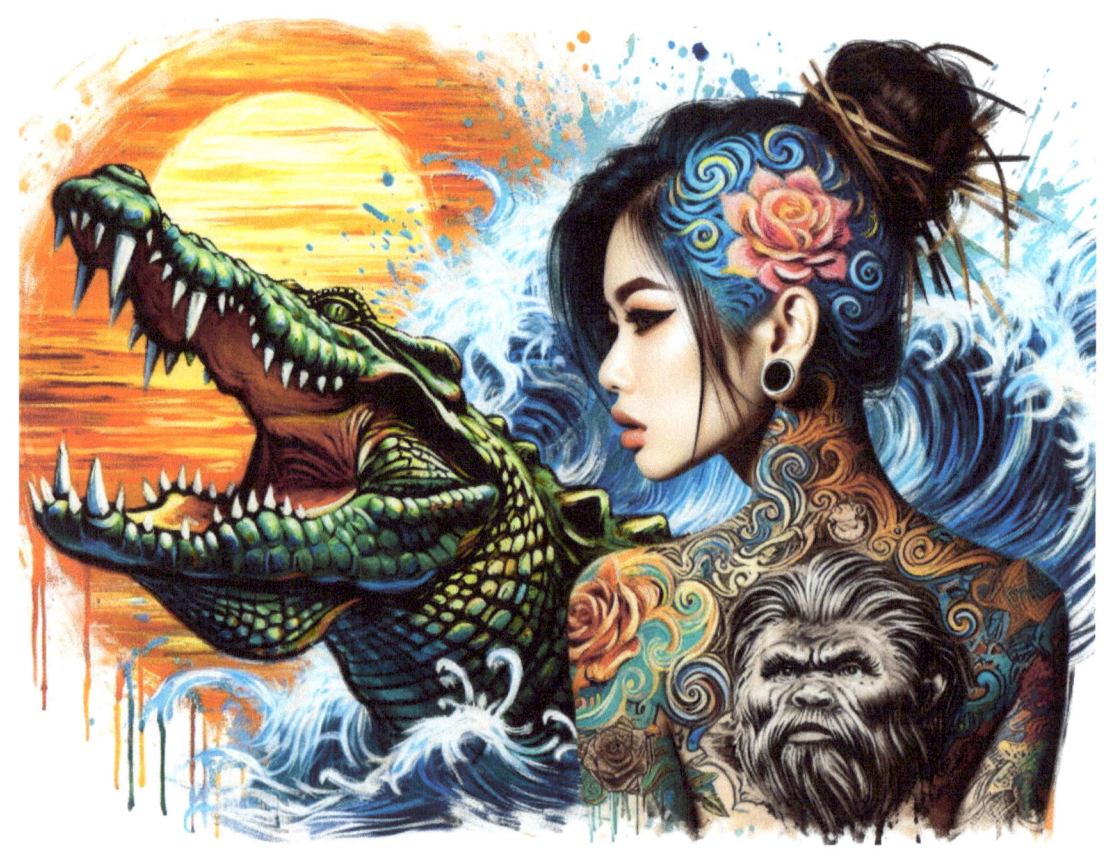

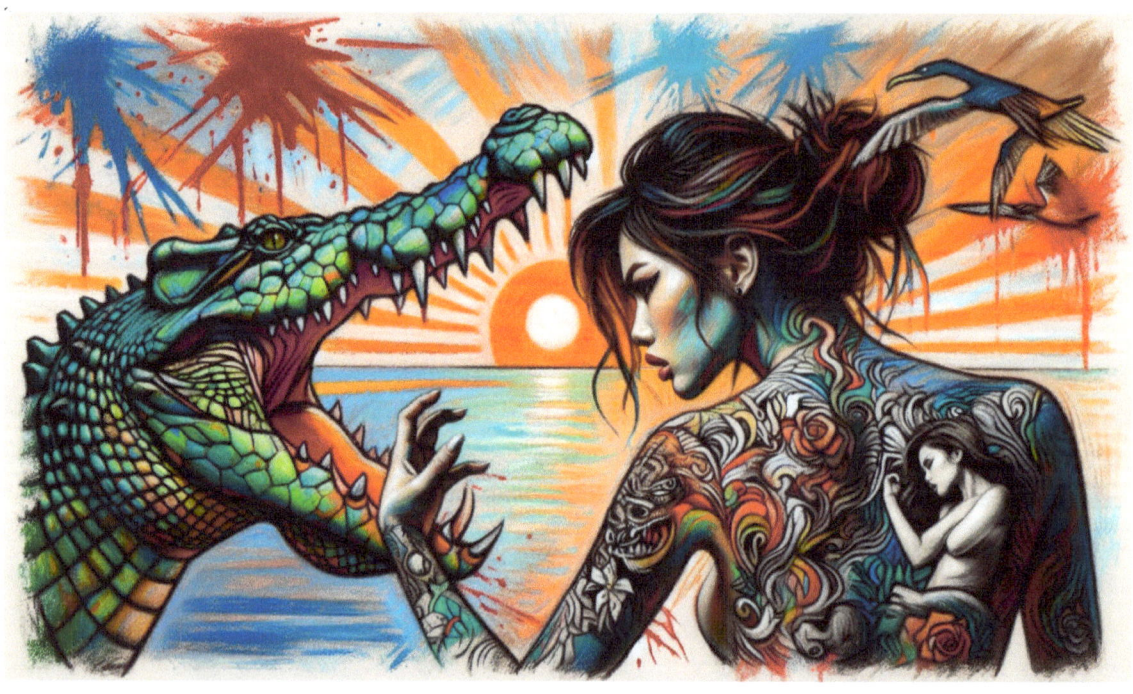

Bird Section

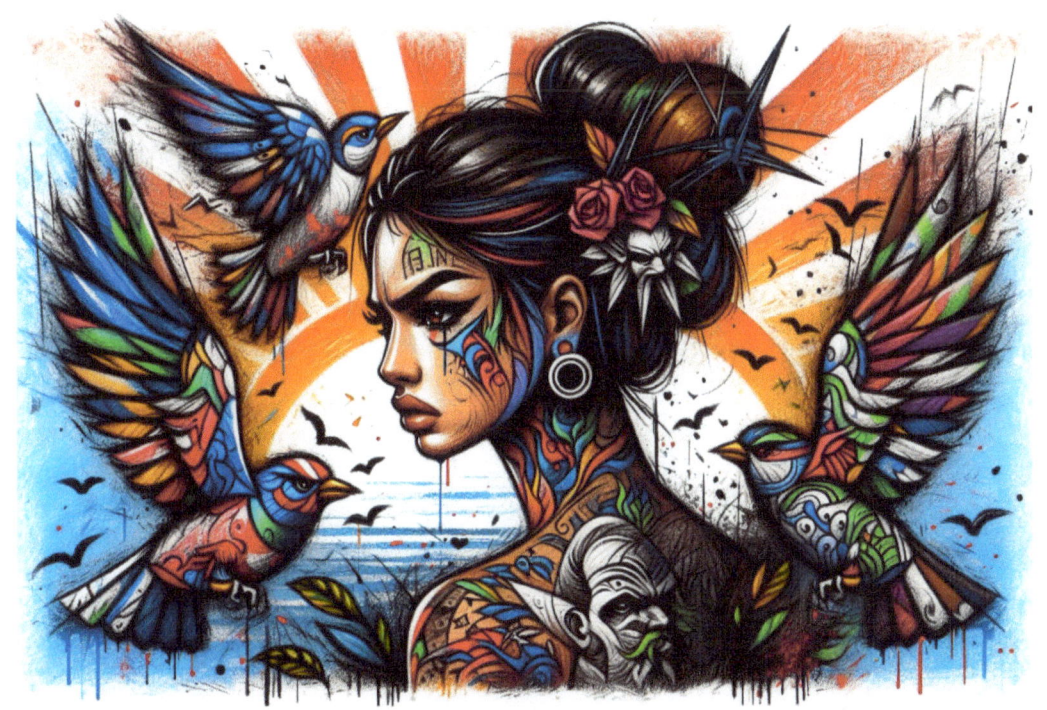

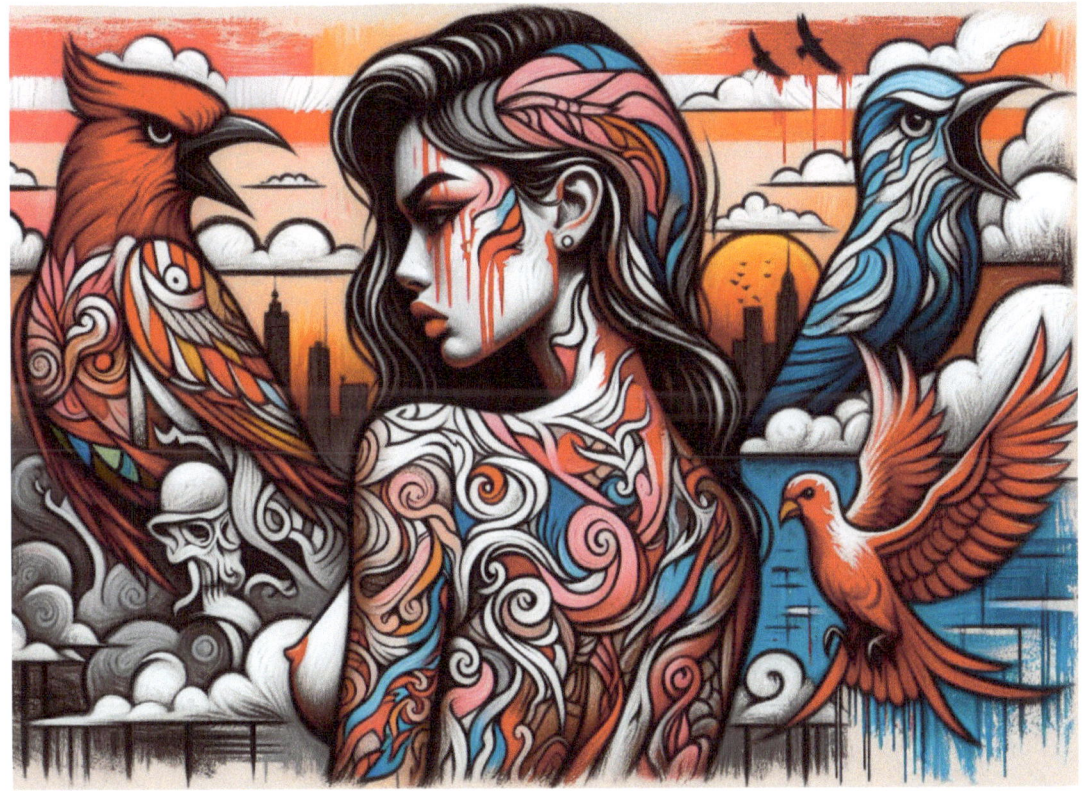

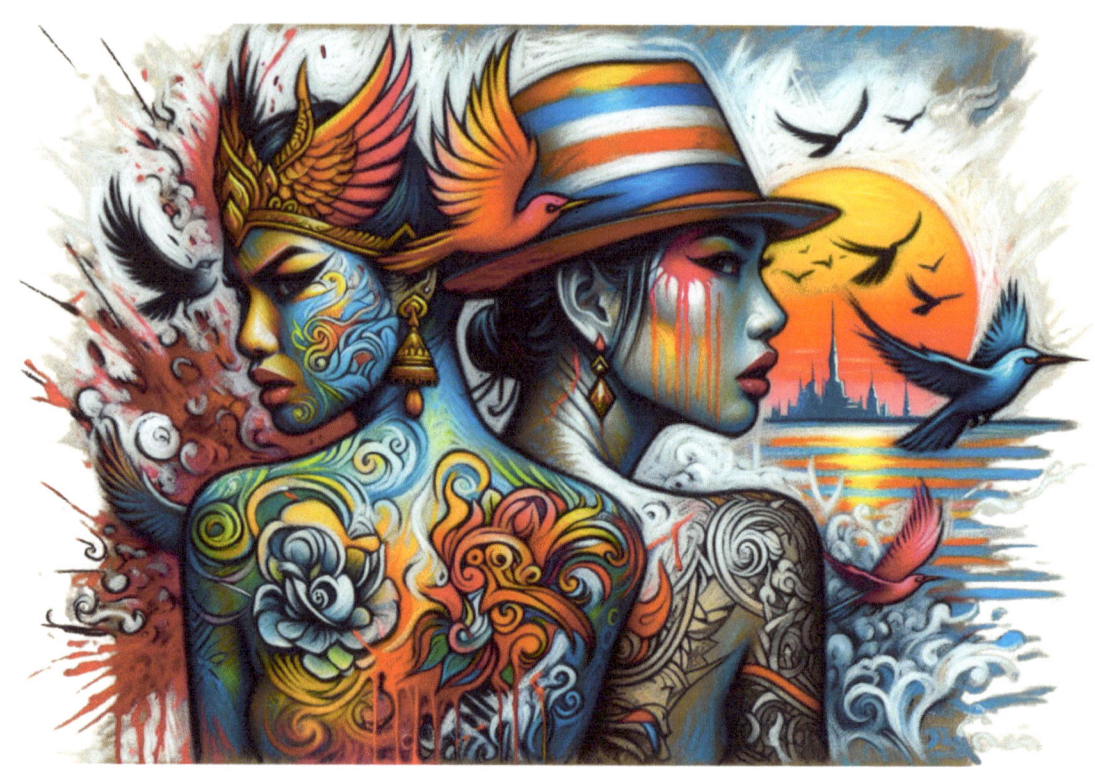

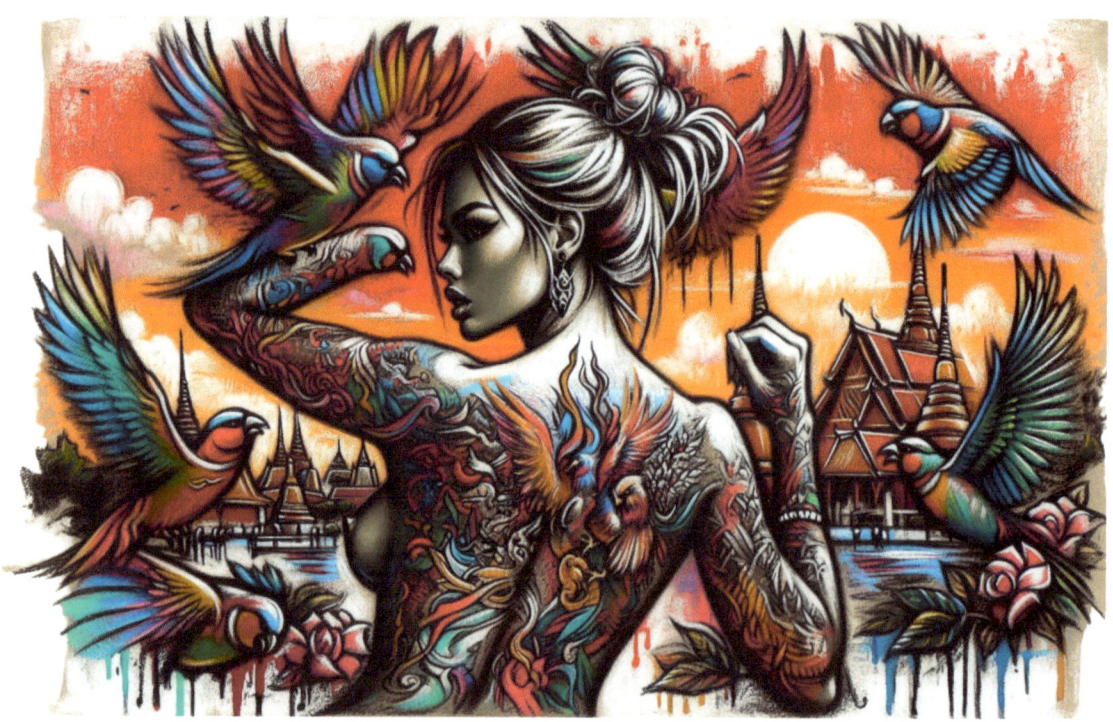

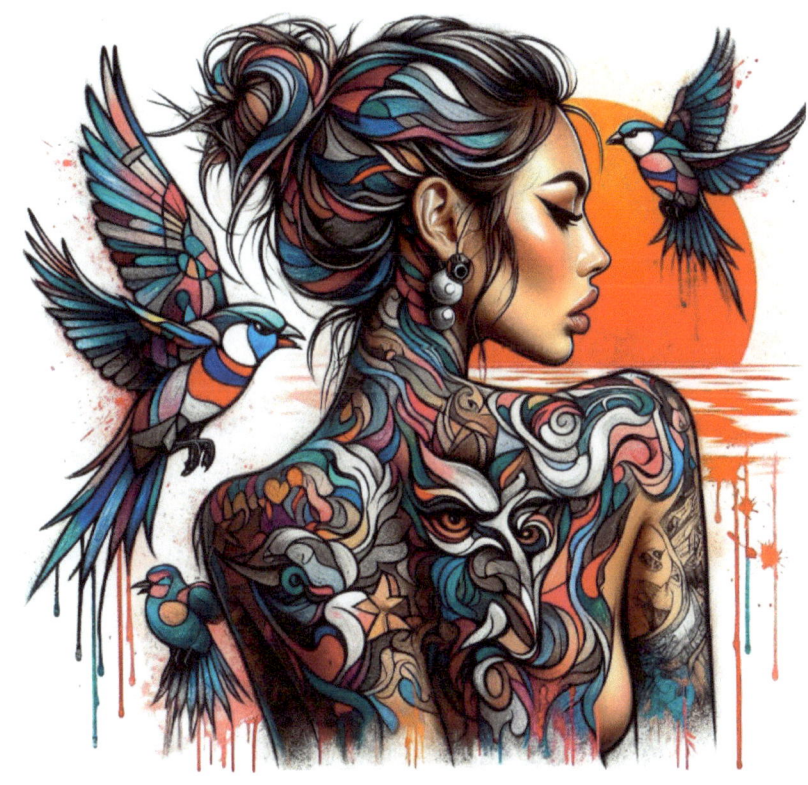

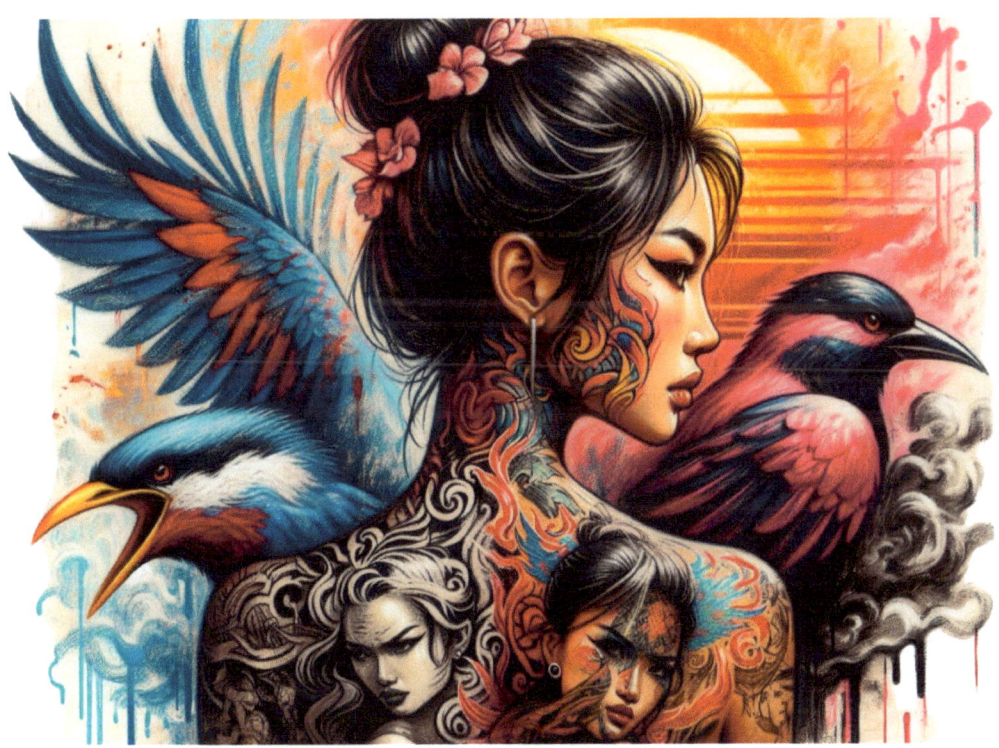

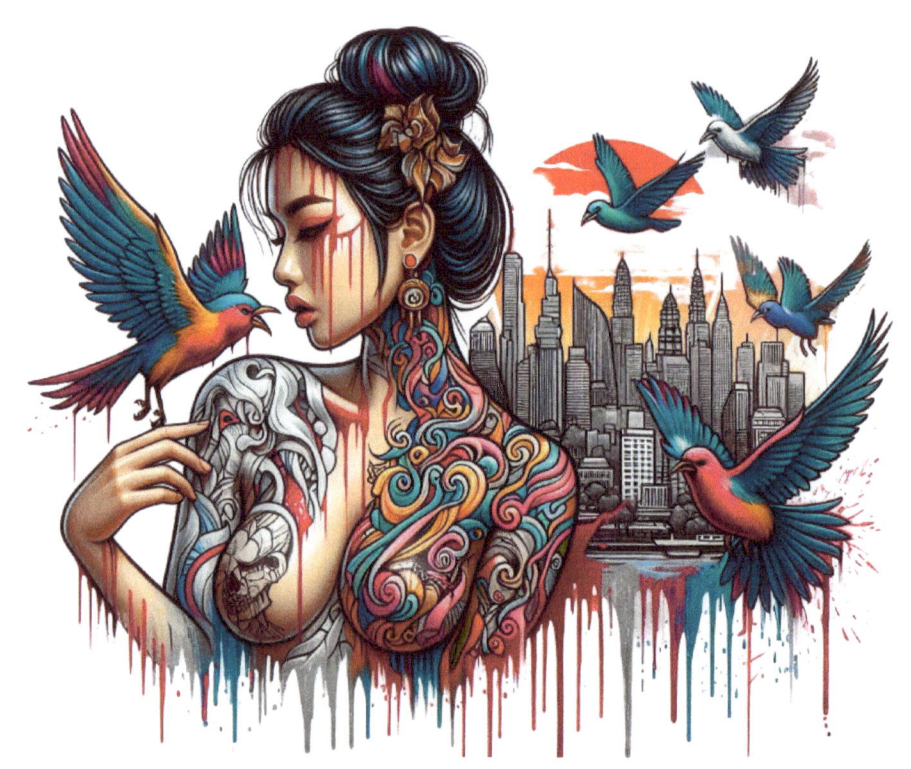

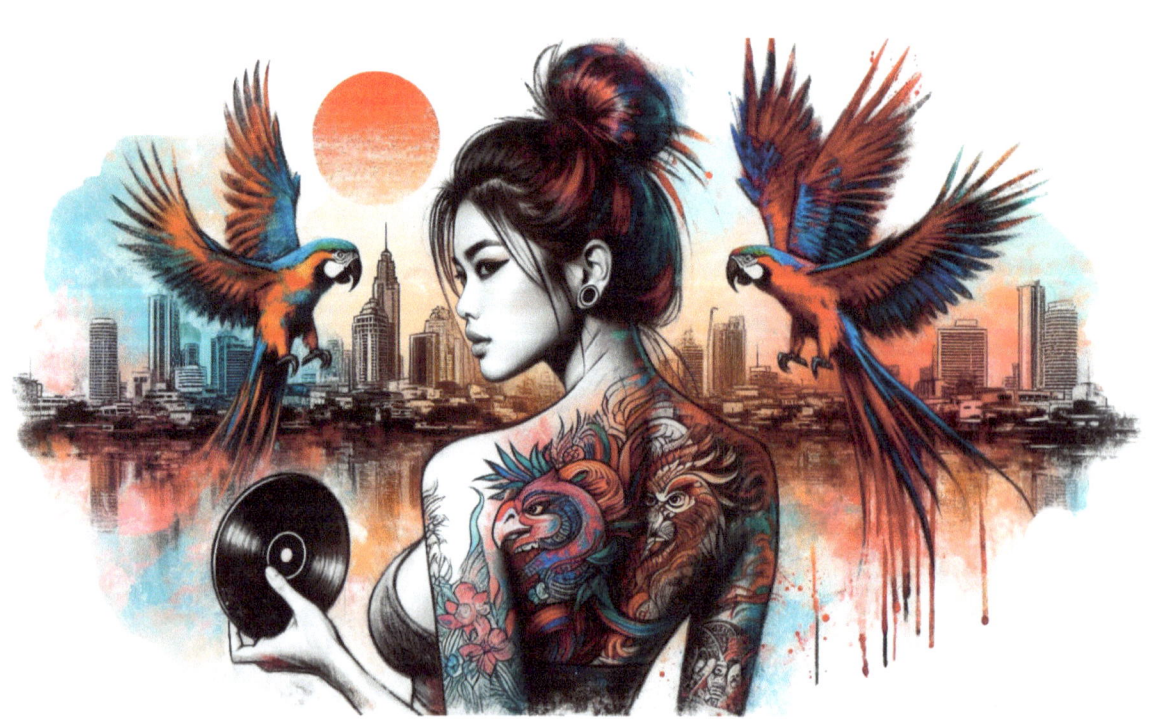

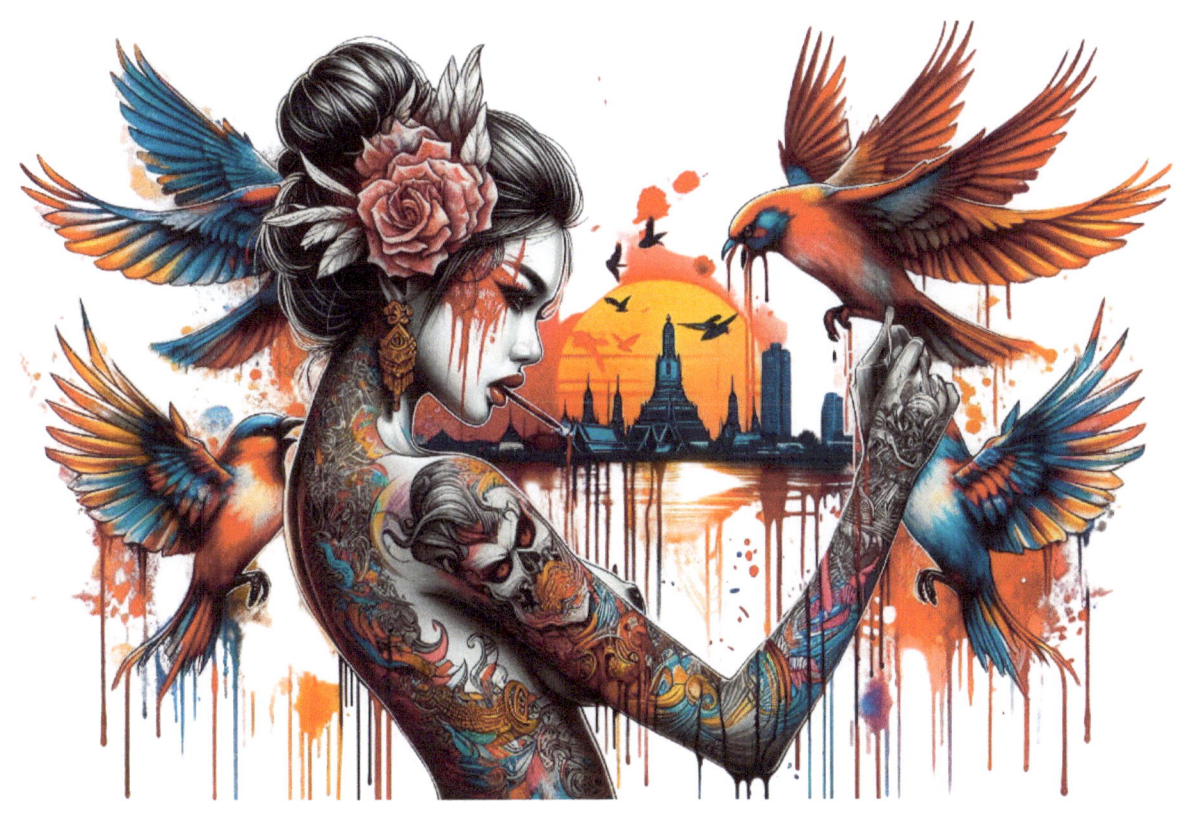

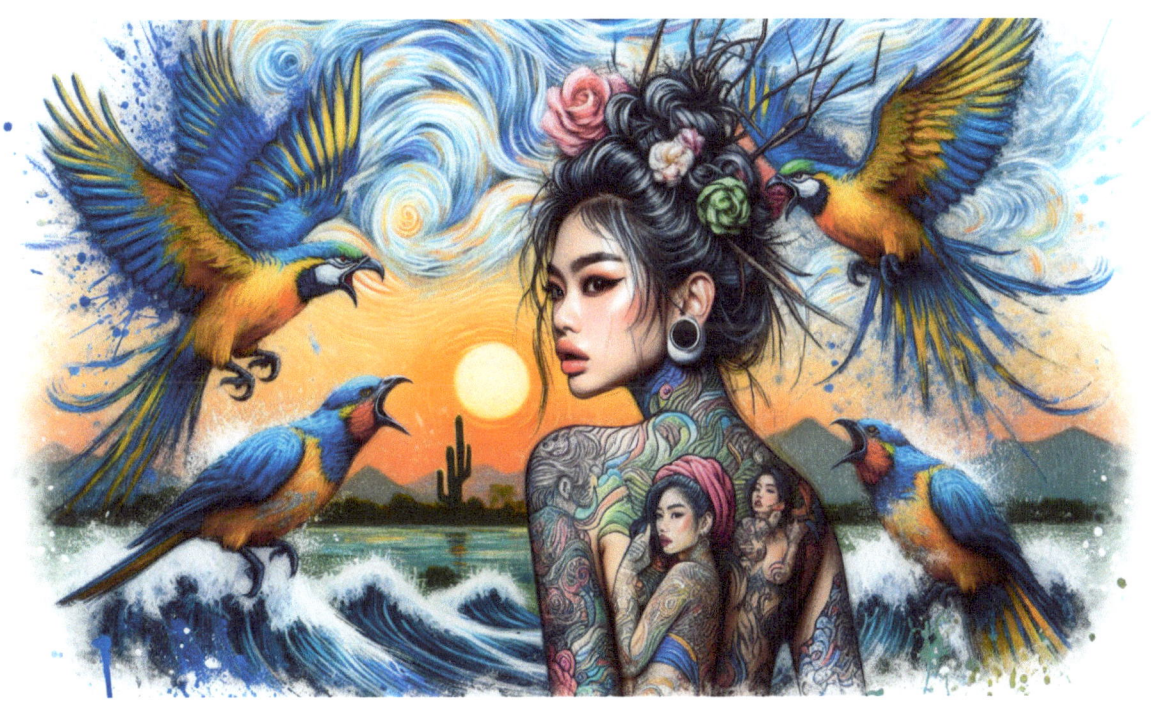

That's it for this Volume. We hope you enjoyed! If we receive enough support we will continue to make License-Free tattoo art available to the world!

https://AmericanRooster.com

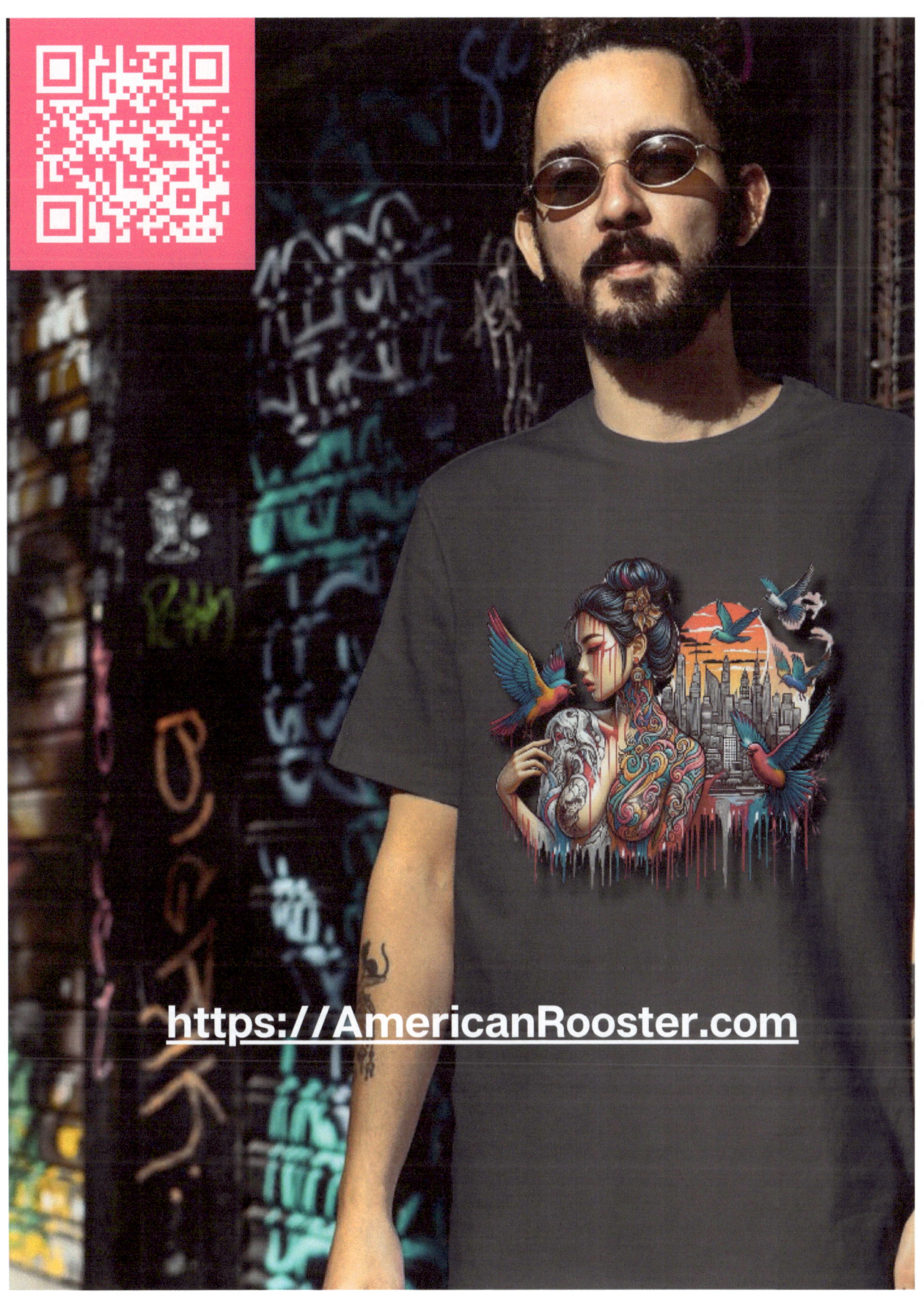

https://AmericanRooster.com